Impacting Lives

Impacting Lives: A Sentimental Journey

Mesa, Arizona

Copyright 2024 Kim Loquai Nielsen

Date of publication: 15 May 2024

ISBN 979-8-9906240-4-7 (hardback)

ISBN 979-8-9906240-0-9 (paperback)

ISBN 979-8-9906240-3-0 (epub)

First Edition

Impacting Lives

A SENTIMENTAL JOURNEY

Kim Loquai Nielsen, RN, BSN

Contents

Business Matters

Reflections

Academia

Preface

I've always been a nurse. Even before receiving my formal education, I cared for and nurtured others. My family, my friends, the neighbors. It was only natural that I would pursue a career in healthcare. Through the years, I transitioned from direct patient care, to managed care, to research. Today my field of study focuses on nutrition.

Though health is my profession, I have always been a writer. From the day my first child was born, I journaled every day until my second child graduated from college. Twenty-four years. Throughout my career, I wrote medical triage guidelines, general medical information guidelines, decision counseling guidelines, policies and procedures, and medical technology assessments for a large managed care organization. I also wrote sections of the solid organ and hematopoietic stem cell transplant guidelines that are in use today.

The formal writing I completed for triage nurses, case managers, and medical directors was reviewed by physician specialists. This book, however, is not intended to be utilized as medical advice or for coverage decisions by individuals or health plans. It's a collection of observations from my profession, my family, and life in general.

Impacting Lives: A Sentimental Journey is a selection of my writings. Musings, memoirs, and opinions, this book represents who I am—how my healthcare experiences and the winding path of my life intersect.

My relationships with others, as expressed in these writings, have been shaped by my vivid life experiences, both good and not-so-good. Yet I've never lost sight of the importance of those who so richly populated my past. They all contributed to who I am and what's important to me.

Kim Nielsen

Whether about healthcare, business, or my spirituality, those experiences, and how I express them in my writing, define me.

When either bold or in doubt, please open and enjoy.

Introduction

My beginnings were inauspicious. I was born Kim Laurie Loquai in Proctor, Minnesota, wherever that is. I have little memory of the experience. My proud French father always told of transporting me home in a laundry basket.

Both my mother and father were raised on Minnesota farms by immigrant parents. From them, I learned the values of family, frugality, being a good steward of what you've been given, and the importance of servant leadership. Both worked hard throughout their lives. I especially remember the "road trips" I took with my father during his traveling sales job in the Midwest. From him I learned the importance of customer service.

I experienced a happy childhood, doing the things most kids did—especially summer vacations at the lakes and on the farms. As I grew into young adulthood, I developed the spiritual commitment I continue today. And I learned how unimportant "fitting in" was. I set my own course while competing as a figure skater, playing trumpet in the jazz band, and enjoying what we now consider simple pleasures.

After graduating from nursing school at Abbott Northwestern Hospital in Minneapolis, I began my long career in nursing, managed healthcare, as well as transplant and medical research. I served as director of nursing at a well-known senior living community. All the while, never wavering from my passion for patient dignity. Today, I continue to research—focusing on nutrition.

I've traveled extensively in the United States, Canada, South America, and Europe—where I visited a toy factory in Germany owned for generations by my dad's family and traveled the route of his family's migration from the Czech Republic and Switzerland.

It's always been important to me to be compassionate to those who need me. And when not doing research or performing service, I love to travel, visit the ocean, cook, listen to music, take long walks, and maintain relationships with my family and lifelong friends. I have a blessed life.

Dedications

I am grateful for God's omnipotence and His faithfulness. I have been blessed with remarkable family, friends, and colleagues, too numerous to list. You know who you are.

Health is Wealth

Chapter 1

Body Defense Mechanisms

October 23, 2023

Food can be the first line of defense for almost every disease. In this discussion, the focus is on disease prevention and treatment through nutrition, not pharmaceuticals. Many physicians state that they only had about a month of nutrition education during medical school. Nevertheless, we can study food as medicine in that health defenses can be activated by the foods we eat.

Based on medical research, there is no such thing as a superfood or super supplement—although that is often how it is marketed. What is super is the human body. Our bodies are hardwired with health defenses that provide what we need to prevent disease, stay fit, improve our health, and recover from illness. The following evidence based medical summaries are backed by science and scientific discoveries about the power of the human body.

Why suppress our health defenses by making it harder for our bodies to stay healthy? What are we doing wrong?

1. Sugar. Adding any sweet (processed) food. Sugar consumption over time overwhelms the body's metabolism and diminishes our health defenses. (Remember, sweet fruits are healthy.)
2. Consuming ultra-processed foods. These are usually found in a box, can, or jar with multiple ingredients—coming from a factory that takes whole foods, grinds them up, colors them, and adds synthetic chemicals. They suppress our body's defenses.
3. Consuming excess alcohol. This practice kills brain cells, liver cells, and puts our health defenses at a disadvantage.

4. Lack of movement. Insufficient exercise turns our microbiome (the collection of bacteria, fungi, viruses, etc., that live on and in our bodies) into an ecosystem that's not efficient and squashes our health defenses. Thirty minutes a day can get blood flowing and change gut microbiome.
5. Overeating. Too much food overwhelms our body's metabolism and health defenses. Our energy is placed into fat cells causing inflammation. *Hara hachi bu* is a Japanese term signifying "Eat until you're 80 percent full."

Below are five health defense systems to recharge and renew us and what we can do to enhance them.

1. <u>Angiogenesis – how our blood vessels are formed.</u> This is important because we have 60,000 miles of blood vessels in our bodies—the highways on which the oxygen gets to cells and organs. But it's important not to have too many blood vessels, because angiogenesis and cancer are linked.

   Angiogenesis is of interest in cancer because cancers require the formation of new blood vessels to grow and metastasize. For cancers to grow to be larger than one millimeter (1 mm), angiogenesis needs to take place. Cancers do this by secreting substances that stimulate angiogenesis. Hence, the growth of cancer.

   Here is an explanation. We are made up of forty trillion cells that are repeatedly dividing, and all human beings have cancers growing microscopically. When we have a healthy angiogenesis defense system, it allows our organs to have circulation but not cancer. However, a mistake can occur when those cells are dividing. It can result in mutations, causing microscopic cancer.

   Such microscopic cancers can grow to the size of a ballpoint pen tip ~ two mm. The reason the cancer can't enlarge is that there is no blood supply delivering oxygen and nutrients. Our angiogenesis blood system prevents this from happening when our immune system defends us by finding those microscopic cancers and eliminating them. The angiogenesis system prevents tumor cells from hijacking good blood vessels to feed themselves. Without a blood supply, those cancers are tiny, pinpoint, and non-threatening.

When angiogenesis defenses are damaged, cancer can grow its own blood supply so that blood vessels grow right up to the tumor and feed it. That cancer can grow rapidly. So, what do we need to do? We need to shore up our ability to prevent extra blood vessels from growing. Although this will never be a problem for most of us, this growth can happen when we compromise our health defenses.

Because tumors cannot grow beyond a certain size or spread without a blood supply, scientists have developed drugs called angiogenesis inhibitors, which block tumor angiogenesis. The goal of these drugs, also called antiangiogenic agents, is to prevent or slow the growth of cancer by starving it of its needed blood supply.

But more than 100 foods also exist that are antiangiogenic and enhance the body's ability to naturally cut off the cancer-feeding blood supply. For example, tomatoes contain lycopene (a bioactive chemical), and human studies show they can reduce the risk of certain types of cancers, including breast and prostate cancer. San Marzano tomatoes have the highest levels of lycopene.

Other antiangiogenic foods, such as black raspberries, cacao, green tea, pomegranate juice, blueberries, walnuts, and soy, cut off the blood supply that feeds breast and other cancers. Soy is another antiangiogenic, cancer-starving food. Soy contains phytosterols, which block estrogen, and has been shown to lower the risk and improve survival in breast cancer.

2. Regeneration. Humans can regenerate tissues naturally using millions of stem cells that occur in many different organs and tissues including the bone marrow, brain, blood, muscle, skin, heart, and liver tissues. Foods can activate this regeneration system by calling out more stems cells, as part of our defense system. For example, long Covid needs stem cells to repair damage. Foods that help with regeneration include dried fruit, 80 percent or more cacao in dark chocolate (with little or no refined sugar), whole wheat, brown rice, barley, oats, and even popcorn. Dietary fiber triggers our stem cells. Sources include swiss chard, mustard greens, collard greens, goji berries (bioactive zeaxanthin), and Chinese celery.

3. Microbiome. We have 39 trillion bacteria in our bodies, primarily beneficial bacteria in the gut. When we eat, whatever nutrients we're

not absorbing in our stomach and intestines travel further down in the intestines to feed our gut bacteria. Gut bacteria help us control our immune system and lower inflammation (important for all chronic diseases). Gut bacteria help heal wounds. Gut bacteria signal the nerves that run between the gut and the brain to release hormones such as oxytocin (feel good hormone), serotonin, dopamine, and GABA.

Certain high fiber, prebiotic foods can improve our microbiome defense system to enhance our brain function and improve mental health. Examples are broccoli, brussel sprouts, kale, kiwi, dark chocolate, mushrooms, and fermented foods.

4. <u>DNA.</u> A health defense system, DNA, primarily protects and codes our entire bodies, although only one to two percent of DNA are protein coding genes. Environmental insults of many varieties contribute to gene mutations, but our DNA is hardwired to repair itself. Alzheimer's disease, autism, cancers, celiac disease, rheumatoid arthritis, cystic fibrosis, depression, diabetes, inflammatory bowel disease, and even PTSD are associated with damaged DNA defenses. Kiwi—the more the better—is a great food to repair DNA.

5. <u>Immune systems.</u> Strong immune systems protect against circulating germs and microscopic cancers. A weakened immune system causes increased disease risks, as seen in immunosuppression, AIDs, autoimmune treatments, and transplants. Inflammation is part of our immune system, but excessive inflammation requires repair to protect immunity. The goal is to decrease inflammation and raise protective immunity (T cells).

Immunotherapy activates the immune system. It's a powerful tool, even when cancer has metastasized. The wall of our gut contains seventy percent of our immune system. MD Anderson together with the NIH studied what makes the difference between melanoma patients who responded to immunotherapy and those who did not. It was found that the responders had a more diverse population of bacteria in the gut or an abundance of certain types of bacteria. Dietary fiber helps grow the types of bacteria that make the difference. Five grams of fiber a day, contained in one pear, can lower risk of cancer growth and mortality by thirty percent.

Another example is mushrooms, which contain a bioactive substance (beta-glucan) that improves immunity. Immunoglobulin A (Ig A, also referred to as sIgA in its secretory form) is an antibody that plays a role in the immune function of mucous membranes. Mushrooms increase these antibodies by as much as fifty percent.

The Cleveland Clinic recently studied seven million subjects and found that Viagra decreased the risk of Alzheimer's disease by sixty-seven percent. The blood vessels in the brain are also dilated by this medicine (nitric oxide increases stem cell regeneration), causing better circulation in the brain. Beets and beet juice also secrete nitric oxide in the bloodstream after swallowing them.

A meta-analysis of dozens of studies looking at nutrition research showed that Vitamin C can dramatically reduce the incidence of many cancers. Oranges, strawberries, guava, red bell pepper, and tomatoes are great sources.

Finally, what foods enhance immunity? Broccoli sprouts (contain isothiocyanates), blueberries (boost T cells), pomegranate juice (antioxidant), chestnuts, blackberries, and walnuts all contribute to our immune health.

Foods that activate all five of the body's defense systems:

Apricots	Mangoes	Peaches
Carrots	Eggplant	Kale
Matcha green tea	Walnuts	Squid ink

Physicians and nutritionists have thousands of pharmaceuticals to treat diseases. But our bodies' health defense systems can be enhanced through nutrition—the foods we eat and don't eat. By managing our intake and emphasizing a select group of foods, we can limit the growth of certain cancer cells, help our bodies regenerate stem cells, improve our microbiome, repair our DNA, and strengthen our immune systems. The human body is more than capable of warding off disease—if we give it the right environment. How about a drink of squid ink?

Chapter 2

Do Vitamin D Levels Matter?

January 23, 2022

Vitamin D is a vitamin that acts as a hormone, with hormone receptors in multiple organ systems, and a common deficiency seen in clinical practice. Low Vitamin D levels cause a significantly reduced quality of life.

Vitamin D deficiency is common in:

chronic low back pain	depression	arthralgias
arthritis	frequent respiratory infections	hair loss
weight gain, obesity	back pain	vegans, vegetarians
Inflammatory conditions	menopausal women	older adults
osteopenia/osteoporosis & other signs of bone loss	living far from equator where there is less sunlight	impaired wound healing after injury or surgery
fatigue syndromes	chronic kidney or liver disease	statin medication use
steroid use	staying indoors regularly	darker skin

The body makes Vit D from cholesterol when your skin is exposed to sunlight. However:

- We are not outdoors as often in sunshine.
- The darker your skin is the more likely you are to be deficient because the melanin in your skin blocks the conversion of the cholesterol from the active form of Vit D (D3).
- Vit D is found in certain foods unpopular in the American diet.
- It is difficult to get adequate Vit D levels through your diet alone.

In pediatric studies, low Vit D levels in children were associated with poor sleep quality and duration as well as delayed bedtime. If your child is having trouble sleeping, it is reasonable to consult their pediatrician and include a Vit D level blood test. In an observational study of female nurses, a strong correlation between fatigue and low Vit D levels was observed. Other studies have shown that supplementing Vit D reduces fatigue.

Because we have such deficiencies in this country, uniform supplementation is recommended. It's been estimated that over one billion people worldwide have low levels of Vit D. In America, it's estimated that about 40 percent of adults are deficient in Vit D while Hispanics are estimated to be 69 percent deficient and African Americans estimated to be 82 percent deficient. Menopausal women have up to 85 percent rates of Vit D deficiency.

Supplementing adults with up to 4000 IU Vit D daily can reduce the risk of respiratory tract infections. Other key benefits of maintaining therapeutic Vit D levels:

- Helps with bone loss, bone pain and back pain
- Increases absorption of calcium from our gut so helps calcium efficiency
- Helps with depression, weight loss, multiple sclerosis, type 2 diabetes, cardiovascular disease
- Keeps immune system strong, helps fight infection
- Increases energy
- Can prevent post-COVID syndrome — also called long-haul COVID, the condition requiring you to be hospitalized if you are deficient in Vit D
- May lower cancer risk

Treatment for Vit D deficiency requires adequate nutrition and Vit D supplementation. However, you cannot supplement poor nutrition! Diet rich in fatty fish, egg yolks, fortified cereals, milk, and juices with Vit D added, yogurt, beef liver, and mushrooms are sources of Vit D.

Vitamin dosages are dependent on whether you need maintenance or are treating a deficiency – which requires a prescription. Vit D supplementation can cause toxicity; therefore, levels need to be monitored to achieve an optimal range. For example, the Endocrine Society recommends that adults take from 1500-2000 IU per day, and others recommend up to 4000 IU per day. Individual metabolism and other factors affect us differently in terms of dose adjustment to achieve therapeutic levels.

There are formulas that may be recommended with Omega 3 and Vit D. If you are allergic to fish, there are brands made from algae (fish eat the algae, which is where they get the Vit D), and vegan or vegetarian brands. The makers of Nordic Naturals claim that "Nordic Naturals Vitamin D3 Vegan is a unique formula specifically developed for vegans and strict vegetarians and is registered by the Vegan Society. Sourced from lichen, this plant-based liquid formula is in the natural form of vitamin D (cholecalciferol) and is a better-absorbed and utilized form of vitamin D."

It is essential to consult with a licensed physician or healthcare professional before beginning any new supplement regimen. A healthcare provider can order appropriate blood tests to monitor levels and ensure that any supplementation is safe and effective for one's specific health profile.

Chapter 3

Compassionate Nurses
October 24, 2022

Earlier today, I found myself reading the employment qualifications for a nursing position. The job description listed a series of competencies that suitable candidates would possess. Among the important qualities mentioned were evidence-based practice, use of informatics, and social justice. Buried among those qualities was sympathetic concern for the sufferings or misfortunes of others: compassion.

I stood at the bedsides of patients who were fearful because they didn't know what was making them so sick. I met people who were dying and families who were raising money from a second or third mortgage to pay for their oncology care. For those individuals, life became a fulltime effort just to seize everything and anything they could to remain hopeful.

In my early days as a nurse, a homeless man I cared for in a county hospital was extremely sick and very apprehensive. I had never seen him before, and he didn't know me. But I cared for him as if he were my father. Afterall, I learned the value of caring at home, from my parents. And he began to trust my concern as he expressed his plight and fears to me. His family noticed his response to compassionate care when his health began to improve. His tearful daughter hugged me tightly and told me that treating her father with dignity was rare and priceless. It reinforced my beliefs that every patient has the same needs and rights, whether a C-Suite executive or someone trying to survive on the street.

Another of my unforgettable patients was a teenage boy who was paralyzed from a spinal cord injury after a fall. His condition was devastating, especially at his early age. I was overwhelmed with compassion for him and spent as much time as I could with him—including my time off. Almost immediately, the boy and his entire family shared their stories, fears, and appreciation. They were receiving more than evidence-based practice, use of informatics or social justice.

It's obviously essential for a patient to receive safe, empathetic care. I haven't done my job if I approach patients in a task-oriented way without seeking to understand and support their individual needs. It's debatable which qualifications are most important for nurses, but individual circumstances dictate how to prioritize safe, therapeutic, compassionate care.

What do you value most in medical care? As a hiring manager, I valued nurses who knew how to listen, knew how to prioritize, knew evidence-based medicine, and demonstrated compassion.

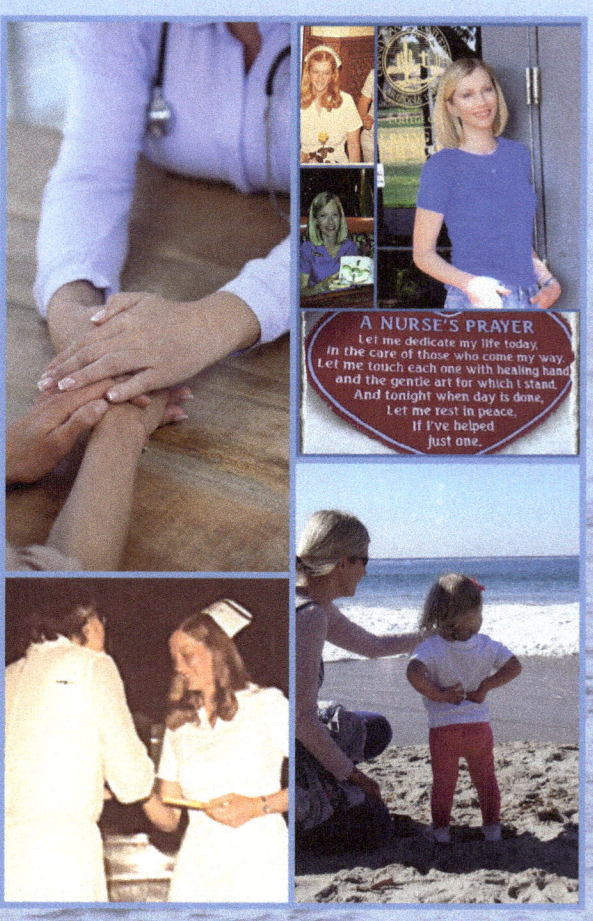

Chapter 4

Lessons Learned from My Practice of Nursing
April 3, 2022

My memories from a career in nursing consist primarily of patients—children and adults who were the subject of my concern, attention, and life's work. But, along with those memories, I took away lessons on patient care which, if asked, I would make part of my personal, nursing training manual.

Care of and respect for my patients, and those who love them, was foundational in my decision to become a nurse. I never forgot that purpose. I tried to be considerate and to treat my patients as I would my own family members and friends—with dignity and respect (regardless of their condition, who they were, or how they treated me).

It took no time to learn that nurses are under intense pressure to perform. Often, nursing teams are short-staffed and called upon to care for more patients than is safe. I learned not to let "efficiency" get in the way of safe and effective care. I always took whatever time was necessary to *prioritize* care.

This includes a lesson on "multitasking" which is an admirable trait in today's demanding society. However, multitasking is a source of safety risk in nursing. Trying to complete more than one task at the same time results in potential inaccuracy and requires more time than if done separately. We know how to walk and chew gum. But try reading and retaining concepts from a pathophysiology textbook while conversing with a friend about her new boyfriend. Then look at the recent trial verdict in the case of RaDonda Vaught in Tennessee. The lesson? Concentrate on one task at a time and do it well.

The pressure on hospital nurses makes taking time for personal care difficult. Yet, it is essential that nurses meet their own needs as well as those of their patients. The airline flight attendants teach us to put on our own oxygen masks first, then help the others around us. You cannot serve others if you do not take care of yourself. I learned when I was providing direct patient care that it was essential for me to allow time to sleep when I went home. A simple, yet essential, lesson.

Do you always leave a visit to your doctor knowing that she or he listened to you? No? It is a common patient complaint. And it is no different for nurses. On occasion, I have been surprised at the lack of listening skills by clinicians. I learned that it's fundamental that I ask questions and "active listen" to patient responses when providing assessments and care. I made it a principle of my care to watch the faces and the bodies of my patients for signs of their needs—another way of listening.

Moreover, I learned to avoid making quick judgments about a patient. Often, they are in great pain, physical or emotional stress, with or without showing it. We rarely know what a patient is really feeling. Just as important, without asking and listening, we cannot be certain what is going on in the patient's life. Is the patient's spouse dying at home? Is the patient's child failing in school? Is their house under foreclosure? These are key factors in listening and determining optimal patient care—to say nothing of providing compassion to the patient. I tried to "walk a mile in the shoes" of my patients while treating them with the same standards I keep for my family.

Finally, as a nurse, I enhanced my leadership skills. A nurse cannot function without being a critical thinker while making on-the-spot decisions that reflect evidence-based medicine—every minute of every day. And no less important, when promoted to leadership positions, I chose a servant leadership style—one who helps other people develop and perform as highly as possible by putting their needs first. My teams flourished, our patients were well-served, and I advanced as a nurse.

My experiences have been emotional yet rewarding, gratifying, and fulfilling. And I was determined to help ease the struggles my patients were experiencing. The lessons I learned made me a more effective nurse.

Chapter 5

Inspirational Textbook

July 14, 2023

I received my initial registered nurse training in a full-time, hospital-based, three-year program. It was an excellent, comprehensive, hands-on education, which left me prepared for my career as a clinical nurse.

Yet, as valuable as that training was, a single textbook stands out as being the most beneficial in my continuing education as a nurse. It was a part of my BSN program and was especially instrumental in my clinical progress: Jarvis, Carolyn, PhD, APN, CNP (2008). *Physical Examination & Health Assessment, International Edition* (5th ed.). Saunders. Dr. Jarvis taught the importance of critical thinking in evaluating specific assessments according to each body system.

Chapter 6

Becoming a Nurse
March 6, 2022

Have you ever considered a career as a nurse? More than three and a half million women and men in the United States are nurses. And the need for nurses continues to grow with more than two hundred thousand new nursing positions expected to be created each year over the next four years. But, aside from employment demand, why become a nurse?

Nursing is a noble profession. Few people are as trusted as nurses. Between 1999 and 2020, an annual Gallup survey of the most trusted professions placed nurses at the top. The only exception? The 2001 survey, in which firefighters took first place. Few other professions combine the academic and clinical skills required of a nurse with the personal compassion that drives most of them.

Becoming a nurse requires extensive formal education and training. That will get you a credential. But nursing requires more. What can't be taught in the classroom is caring and empathy. A nurse is called to the profession out of a personal need to care for others. Florence Nightingale, who founded the first school of nursing, believed that God called her to nursing.

Initially, nurses were little more than family caretakers with no formal education. Then, in 1860, St. Thomas Hospital in London, England, began the formal training of nurses under the direction of Ms. Nightingale. Originally, only women were nurses. By 2021, there were more than one thousand nursing schools in the United States educating more than two hundred fifty thousand nursing students each year. More than nine percent of nurses were male.

Beyond the "calling," what is it that draws people to nursing? There are two clear opportunities for people in the nursing profession. First, there are a variety of career options open to nurses. No longer does being a nurse mean only caring for sick patients in a hospital. Today, nurses have the option of working in hospitals, long-term care facilities, clinics, physician's offices, prisons, from home, as a traveling nurse in hospitals across the country, and in other specialty roles. Many nurses work at desks in businesses.

Second, the compensation is good. According to the U.S. Bureau of Labor Statistics, the 2019 median salary for a Registered Nurse was seventy-three thousand dollars. However, the five highest-paying states for nurses in the U.S. list average salaries that fluctuate between ninety-one and one hundred six thousand dollars, depending on location, experience, specialty, certifications, and education.

If you feel the calling to care for people and the willingness to work hard for your credential, consider a career as a nurse. If you do, you are bound to be richly rewarded.

Chapter 7

Choosing a BSN Program
March 6, 2022

The healthcare field is a rapidly evolving environment, and nurses need in-depth preparation and training before handling professional responsibility as an RN. As baby boomers age, state populations are seeing an increase in residents over 65. In fact, those over 85 will be the most rapidly growing age group. This increase in the ratio of seniors will lead to more elderly patients who statistically need more intensive medical care services.

Different careers require specific levels of training and education. When it comes to health care, rigid expectations are put in place to keep patients safe. The nursing profession is both demanding and rewarding. Nurses trained with a BSN degree are more prepared to meet those demands compared to nurses with an associate's degree. Technically, an associate degree in nursing (ADN) qualifies you to take the National Council Licensure Examination (NCLEX) to earn an RN license and become a registered nurse. But hospitals today prefer nurses with a Bachelor of Science in nursing (BSN).

A top school of nursing will provide a challenging program that prepares you to practice as a registered nurse. The BSN takes around four years to complete with full-time education. Courses cover the same general education requirements and healthcare classes as the ADN, plus added courses on science, math, leadership, and public health. The BSN-prepared nurse is sought-after in the job market because of their in-depth training. While some students choose to get an ADN, the two-year degree will later require an RN to BSN program to advance into a higher position within the healthcare field. If you want to become a leader in nursing or plan to eventually get your master's degree, you will need to join an RN to BSN program to first get a higher degree than an ADN.

Baccalaureate programs provide full-time classes and clinical experiences before their students graduate and take the NCLEX. Taking the NCLEX is required to practice as a registered nurse. High pass rates will tell you some important things about a prospective program. For example, a high NCLEX pass rate is advantaged by having hands-on training, a high-quality curriculum, top-caliber faculty, ample preparation for testing, and supportive faculty.

A top nursing college or university will typically promote their own NCLEX pass rate. However, when looking into a nursing school that does not clearly show their NCLEX pass rate, it can be found on the website for the state's board of nursing. These websites list the pass rates by school. Check the scores of schools you are interested in and investigate how they performed over the last five years. According to the National Council of State Boards of Nursing (NCSBN), the national first time NCLEX-RN pass rate for U.S. educated nurses in 2020 was eighty-six percent. Prospective nursing students should choose a school that consistently ranks at or higher than the national average.

It's also important to take a close look at the professors in your RN program, because they will choose the materials you will be taught, and they will be the ones to determine your grades. Great programs have highly qualified nurses with their master's or doctorate degree. While a BSN is needed to teach in the college setting, most schools expect higher degrees to ensure that their nursing professors are prepared to instruct in a variety of courses and topics.

The National Council of State Boards of Nursing (NCSBN) recommends that faculty have a master's degree or a doctorate in nursing when teaching at an academic level. It is important that all educators hold a higher mastery of the class than their students. Whether in person or online RN classes, the professor must be able to masterfully teach the material and help students achieve a depth of understanding. If professors are not well prepared or highly educated, they will train nurses that fall short of the expectations of collegiate nursing education.

Quality of Clinical Partnerships

Look into where the university carries out its nursing training for clinical hours and other on-site opportunities. Make sure your chosen school has a connection with reputable hospitals and organizations where you can get these professional experiences. You do not want to put a lot of effort into classes, only to have substandard clinical experience.

You can usually find out where a school has their clinical hours. The relationships with community healthcare facilities will tell you a lot about the caliber of the school. Look at the facilities where they send students and decide if it looks like a good fit and a valuable experience.

Chapter 8

My Influencers

October 10, 2022

When we look back on our careers, we realize we have interacted with hundreds, even thousands, of people. People who were our colleagues, our customers, our suppliers, our teachers, our students, our bosses, our subordinates, and/or our friends. There were others.

Certain individuals we interacted with are distant memories. Whatever their relationship to us might have been, they came and went without influence. But others did. And for me, an even smaller group did so in rare form. They had so much impact on me that I think of them regularly, though I may not have seen or talked to them in years. They remain my influencers.

The impressive individuals who influenced me were a profound source of inspiration to me and others. I remember something important that each of them taught me. I was more effective in my career as a nurse because of them. They share my values, and they are caring and generous servant leaders. In their own unique ways, they are all champions.

Now, it's your turn. Who inspired you? Who helped shape you into the professional you are? Remind yourself of those you have never forgotten. Give public credit to those to whom you are grateful for the effect they had on you and your career. I trust that you will experience gratitude all over again.

Chapter 9

Dietary Supplement Decisions

April 8, 2023

Interpreting medical information to make health care decisions is seldom clear-cut. Scientists make recommendations. Experts don't always agree. Sources may or may not be reputable. Profit motives, promises of unproven results, and persuasive salespeople (fake experts), can deceive the public.

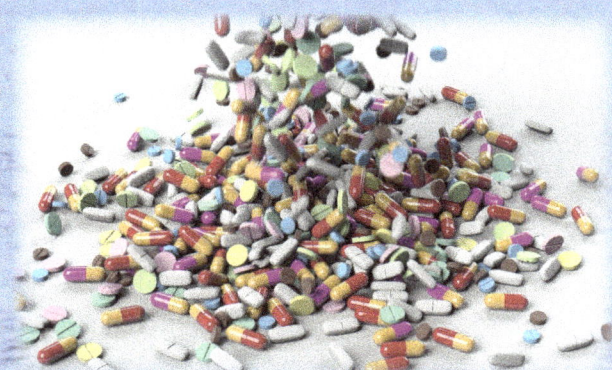

Image by Arek Socha from Pixabay

Choosing safe and effective supplements depends on knowing age-appropriate, evidence-based, up-to-date medical findings that consider individual health status. Yet, who are the trusted medical experts? What is a safe dosage? When are results expected? Are over-the-counter supplements subject to quality control? All products are not equal.

People commonly consume high doses of certain nutrients but are deficient in others. Fortunately, nutritional testing is available to identify individual needs. Talk to your primary physician to determine proper testing options based on your health needs.

Chapter 10

Wearable, Ingestible, and Implantable Technologies
November 4, 2022

A great deal is being written about healthcare "wearables." These devices are designed to be worn on the body to monitor, improve, or report health status. Depending on your choice, devices can measure blood oxygenation, blood pressure, heart rate, calories burned and/or your sleep—to name a few. They might even order your Starbucks. Garmin Pay allows you to make purchases with a quick tap. Such lightweight microelectronics make possible a variety of health enhancing applications. But, along with wearables, internal implants are available for almost every body part.

Health improvements utilizing innovative technology are not new. The first wearable eyeglasses are believed to have been invented in Italy during the late 13th century, though there is dispute as to whom credit should be given. The concept is unchanged today although eyeglasses have been enhanced via bifocals, contact lenses and frame technology.

The evolution of hearing aids is more complicated. Beginning with large ear "trumpets" in the 17th century, electronic devices, using early tube-type radios, followed in the 1920s. Then came transistorized versions in the 1970s, which were still quite clumsy. The first digital device, a precursor to today's technology, required a body-worn processor connected to the earpiece. In contrast, today's digital hearing aid is almost invisible and can be linked to a smart phone or computer.

As a Minnesota trained nurse, I recall that Earl E. Bakken developed the first wearable transistorized pacemaker in 1957—at the request of the well-known heart surgeon Dr. C. Walton Lillehei. Earlier pacemakers were AC-powered, so this battery-powered device liberated patients from power-cord alternatives. The new device was a forerunner to today's fully contained, implantable pacemakers.

In the mid 1990's the cardiac loop recorder, an implantable recording device which is inserted under the skin near the heart, was released as a diagnostic tool to evaluate cardiac arrhythmias with otherwise unexplained episodes of syncope. An implantable loop recorder can capture information that a standard electrocardiogram or Holter monitor may miss, such as arrhythmias that are brief or infrequent.

But what about today? Technology is readily available in wristwatches, armbands, and bracelets to accomplish any number of monitoring and diagnostic functions 24 hours a day, every day. Oxygen saturation, glucose levels, and vital signs are examples of measurements which can be observed and recorded. With an appropriate connection, a healthcare provider can be notified immediately in the event of an abnormality.

In addition to health technology that is worn on the body today, there are microcomputers which can either be swallowed or placed under the skin to perform the same functions as the wearables plus new ones. The next sensor might be inside you rather than on you. Imagine a pill which could survive inside the body and convey information. Scientists believe that tiny capsules will be able to communicate data, for example to measure glucose levels, or transmit photos of the interior of organs. It might also confirm to your doctor that you took your prescription medications or measure your body's response to that medication. A technology called capsule endoscopy utilizes a tiny camera to allow a doctor to see the inside of a patient's colon. Colon capsule endoscopy is considered by many to be a viable alternative to colonoscopy (for the investigation of intermediate and low-risk patients with gastrointestinal symptoms).

There are some negatives to emerging technology. Not surprising, there are mechanical errors and malfunctions. It is one thing if a provider is notified, in error, that blood pressure is high. But what happens when the provider is notified that blood pressure is normal when it is, in fact, dangerously elevated? A life could be at stake. What happens when a user is exercising at a dangerous heart rate, but the device reports it as normal?

Then, there is the matter of data security. These devices not only hold substantial health data, but they are frequently linked to financial and personal data as well. The integrity of that data and the privacy of that patient could be at risk.

Finally, not everyone is willing to have a device implanted under their skin. Researchers found that patients are skeptical as to the usability of such technology, they fear health risks, and are uncertain of results and costs. In addition, there is wide variability of acceptance based upon demographic characteristics such as age, immigration status, personality traits and health status.

I was part of a policy review group in the late '70s which evaluated an implantable glucose infusion pump. Similar pumps remain in wide use. A 2018 article by the FDA describes artificial pancreas device systems that closely mimic the glucose regulating function of a healthy pancreas. Most artificial pancreas device systems consist of technology already familiar to many people with diabetes: a continuous glucose monitoring system (CGM) and an insulin infusion pump. Blood glucose devices (such as a glucose meter) are used to calibrate the CGM.

Ingestibles and implantables are the product of the genius of physicians, scientists, and engineers who imagine, conceive, and create healthcare solutions beyond the imagination of most of us. We benefit from them when a doctor deems it necessary. But wearables are a personal decision. We can buy a smart watch this afternoon. If you were born before 1970, could you have even imagined 'smart' stethoscopes, robots powered by artificial intelligence, digital inhaler devices, or artificial eye lenses?

Chapter 11

Financial and Personal Health Go Hand in Hand
January 12, 2022

We can always find reasons for concern—both about financial matters and health matters. Even when things are stable, we may feel tentative. What could go wrong?

Well, any number things, it would seem. In recent years, to name a few on the financial front, we have had irrational exuberance, reluctance to accept election results, the feared collapse of Greece, the attacks on America in 2001, and the financial crisis of 2008. Today, we have increased inflation, rising interest rates, the relentless spread of COVID-19, excessive asset valuations, and soaring government debt. Of course, a lot goes right as well. Since the 3rd quarter of 2020, the economy has continued to grow. Unemployment is at an all-time low. Personal savings are up dramatically. Good jobs are plentiful. Until weeks ago, the stock market was at an all-time high.

Wall Street often encounters what it calls the "Wall of Worry" – a collection of negative factors potentially affecting the price of stocks. Falling prices during the early weeks of 2022 offer an example. Can the price of stocks overcome the wall of worry and the various economic, social, and geopolitical factors that influence them? And what does it mean for our health? How should we climb the wall of worry?

Worrying about anything can affect our health. COVID-19 is unlikely to go away. Nor will influenza. Do we worry too much? An article in Harvard Health entitled "Always worried about your health?" describes a condition known as Health Anxiety Disorder. It's useful information.

Despite skepticism and debate, the COVID-19 vaccine is appraised as a scientific breakthrough for providing protection to hundreds of millions of people. Advances in robotic surgery are found to increase precision and shorten recovery time. Artificial pancreas technology, approved by the FDA, is showing improvements in blood glucose control for diabetics. Pioneers of Alzheimer's disease are finding effective ways to treat symptoms of cognitive decline. This list goes on. We are living longer.

So, how should we choose to approach the wall of worry? Afterall, it is a choice. How we do so reflects our tolerance for risk and our confidence that things will resolve themselves. We can be paralyzed by the thought of the things we face – plunging stock prices, dread disease, or otherwise. Or we can recognize those things for which we have control and act on them. Those we cannot control we leave in the hands of someone who can.

If we are worried about potentially lower stock prices, we can lower our stock allocation or get out of the market altogether. If not, we can leave things alone and allow prices to recover. If we are worried about our health, we can address it by improving our diet, consulting with specialists, exercising, and acknowledging our own tendency to be anxious—making personal health a priority. If not, we can go on enjoying our lives as usual.

It is up to us how we climb the wall of worry. Faith over fear.

Chapter 12

Wellness

October 25, 2023

Wellness is not a passive or static state. Being well is associated with intentions, choices, and actions that contribute to an optimal state of health.

Last evening, I took a long walk in unsupportive flipflops. The next morning, I woke up with aching feet. Inflammation is a normal response to injury (or pathogens) that allow the body to heal itself. I proceeded to stretch and soak my feet in an Epsom salt foot bath. Then, I sought out some restorative recipes in a publication called Eat to Beat Inflammation. Each recipe included some of the top inflammation fighting foods, along with the healing power of spices.

Kim Nielsen

We know that inflammation is the root of several chronic diseases, so understanding which foods calm inflammation and which contribute is important to making healthy food choices. Chronic inflammation is triggered by environmental compounds, the food we eat, stress, smoking, and/or inadequate sleep. Chronic inflammation can eventually damage cells and overwork the immune system, leading to serious chronic conditions.

So, after perusing the recipes I decided to test another one for lunch today. I added salmon and dill sauce to the "White Beans and Tomatoes with Kale Pesto" recipe. It was delicious and turned out to be a favorite! Anti-inflammatory nutrition is known for being rich in antioxidants, omega-3 fatty acids, healthy fats, polyphenol-rich foods, and herbs & spices.

Healthy practices do not have to be boring or repetitious. There is plenty to learn and a wealth of creative choices.

Chapter 13

Spiritual Health
January 9, 2023

Anxiety and Depression in Society

Nurses encounter an alarming level of anxiety and depression among their patients. According to data from the 2022 Centers for Disease Control and Prevention, 27.3% of Americans aged eighteen and older have symptoms of an anxiety disorder. Alarming concerns are everywhere. Political chaos, unsatisfying jobs, the pandemic, and doubt about the economy and/or the future. The list goes on.

The Journal of the AMA cited a study that shows an exponential increase in anxiety and depression. People of each generation in the 20th century were three times more likely to experience depression and anxiety than people of preceding generations. To see the consequences of anxiety, just read about half the ailments in any medical textbook.

Why? We are safer now than ever. Healthcare is better. We regulate food, water, electricity, and businesses. We have police and fire protection. Emergency medical care is minutes away. Few of us live under the threat of physical harm. Yet if worry were an Olympic event, the US would win the gold medal.

In a study of more than 200,000 incoming college first-year students, students report an all-time low in overall mental and emotional stability. Psychologist, Robert Lahey, pointed out that the average child today exhibits the same level of anxiety as the average psychiatric patient of the 1950s.

So, when treating a patient, how does a nurse respond to these realities?

Spiritual Health

Experts have defined spiritual health as a dimension of human wellness that integrates all other dimensions of health: physical, emotional, financial, and social. So, where does spiritual health fit into physical health and well-being and, specifically, anxiety and depression? And how can a nurse give spiritual comfort to her patient?

The Word of God teaches us that Paul experienced hardship, enemies, debilitating physical ailments, opposition to his ministry, prison time, angry mobs, and shipwrecks. He encountered adversity every step of the way. It's the same with us. As soon as we try to ascend and build something in the kingdom of God, the enemy comes in to tear down what we're trying to build. Is the Lord closing the door or is the enemy blocking our way?

Nurses encounter patients with severe anxiety or depression every day. That can be debilitating enough. But, often, there is another cause. The patient may be seeking comfort apart from their presenting symptoms/condition. Financial difficulty, loss of a job, sickness in the family, an abusive relationship and losses may add significant stress to an already anxious patient.

When the door to the solution hasn't opened yet, it could simply be a matter of timing. Or it could be a matter of spiritual commitment. We don't always know. Is this a test of faith, or is God using the opposition to redirect us right where He wants us to go?

An effective tool to deal with anxiety or depression is gratitude (as soon as you acknowledge your blessings, the trepidations can become less intense). The more grateful one's heart is, the less anxious the soul. A nurse can comfort a patient by encouraging them to identify their blessings. Ask your patients what blessings they appreciate most. A loving spouse? Food in the refrigerator? A warm bed in which to sleep? Healthy grandchildren? Sufficient skills to secure employment?

The Bible directs us to order our lives in a way that honors the Lord as He promises to direct our steps. If God is sovereign over the universe, isn't He able to help us overcome what keeps us up at night? A patient's fear triggers either prayer or despair, and the nurse can help them choose wisely.

Nurses play a critical role in the physical health of their patients. But they are also important in maintaining the spiritual health of their patients. Although it is tempting to oversimplify such matters, if we were as committed to our spiritual workout as our physical workout, we could enhance our spiritual health dramatically. By encouraging patients to seek spiritual comfort, nurses help assure the integration of all dimensions of human wellness.

Chapter 14

Screen Time

December 11, 2021

Protecting children is one of life's worthiest causes. My experience as a manager of triage nurses specializing in pediatric care reinforced the obvious vulnerability of infants and children. They depend on us. And they need us to be engaged with them.

Erika Christakis, an early childhood educator and a widely published graduate of Harvard College with master's degrees in education and public health, has important insight into the relationship between child development and smartphone screen time. In her article in the July 2018 edition of The Atlantic, she presented research on the subject. Though her article is three years old, it is, to me, more relevant today than it was when first published.

Interestingly, Erika is not talking about children's use of smartphones. She concludes, "More than screen-obsessed young children, we should be concerned about tuned-out parents." That is, she sees more damage to child development from parents being on the phone or working the keyboard than from a child's use of a smart device. She reports that while parents are "…actually spending more time with children than their parents did, the interactions are of increasingly low-quality…." Use of smartphones is a significant cause.

Erika quotes Kathy Hirsch-Pasek from a published study, "Language is the single best predictor of school achievement, and the key to strong language skills are those back-and-forth fluent conversations between young children and adults…. Toddlers cannot learn when we break the flow of conversations by picking up our cellphones or looking at the text that whizzes by our screens."

There are important messages in this article. And there are people we know who should learn from them. Read the article and pass it along. Children need us, and they are not responded to when we are on the phone, texting, or reading messages.

Christakis is sympathetic to the demands on parents to be "all things to all people." But her concluding comment does more than just summarize her article:

> "Parents should give themselves permission to back off from the suffocating pressure to be all things to all people. Put your kid in a playpen, already! Ditch that soccer-game appearance if you feel like it. Your kid will be fine. But when you are with your child, put down your damned phone."

It is a call to action.

Chapter 15

Laughter

March 23, 2024

Do you know people who are unaffected by stress? Your five-year-old child, for example? Are you looking for the silver bullet? Well, you might have just found one—a good laugh.

The only cohort of people as large as those who feel stress might be those who have heard advice on how to lower stress. And here's more advice.

Today, I read an article by three behavioral scientists who say, "Nothing works faster or more dependably to bring your mind and body back into balance than a good laugh." And they claim that laughter strengthens the immune system. So, laugh your way out of stress and into improved health!

Why is this important? There is abundant evidence that chronic stress plays a part in heart disease, diabetes, and the aging process. According to a special report published by Harvard Health Publications, manage stress, and see improvements such as lowered blood sugar, improved cardiac function, and weight loss (laughter burns calories!).

Okay. But what if you're worrying so much you can't bring yourself to laugh or otherwise manage stress? In an article by the same behavioral scientists who wrote about laughter, entitled The Effects of Worry and Anxious Thoughts by Lawrence Robinson, Melinda Smith, M.A., and Jeanne Segal, Ph.D., the authors claim "Chronic worrying is a mental habit that can be broken. You can train your brain to stay calm and look at life from a more balanced, less fearful perspective."

Life is short. Consider using the four As recommended 2/1/21 by the Mayo Clinic:

Avoid: "Believe it or not, you can escape some minor stressors by taking control of your situation. Find ways to make things better. For instance, if your commute is stressful, consider listening to a new CD to make it more enjoyable. Create physical distance from stressors, such as avoiding a co-worker who continually irritates you. Learn to say no when necessary."

Alter: "Take inventory of your stressors and attempt to change your situation for the better. Clearly communicate your expectations to others. Respectfully ask someone to alter how they treat you. Use "I" statements to express your feelings. State your limitations in advance, like saying, "I only have five minutes to talk.""

Accept: "Sometimes, despite our efforts, we must accept things as they are. Talk to someone about your feelings—call a friend, have coffee with a relative, or schedule an appointment with a therapist. Forgiveness is essential for accepting stressful situations and moving forward."

Adapt: "Change your standards and expectations regarding stress. Don't strive for perfection; instead, make reasonable substitutions in your daily life. Focus on positive aspects and avoid replaying stressful situations in your mind. Ask yourself if the stressor will matter in five years to gain perspective."

And if you are serious about learning how the body and mind are connected, there is an online course presented by Harvard Medical School about the mind-body connection. Check it out on the HMS website. And what do you know, there are three breakout sessions addressing humor as therapy at Harvard Medical School! Start laughing now and you won't need it.

> *"I don't trust anyone who doesn't laugh."*
> - Maya Angelou

Chapter 16

Social Isolation
February 20, 2022

Two years ago, this month, we began the nation's battle against what we now know as the Coronavirus (COVID-19) pandemic. Over 78 million cases in the United States and more than 930 thousand deaths later, the effects are still with us. People are still wearing masks, and many are still staying home.

In increasing numbers, employees have shifted their worksite from an office to their home. We're told the "hybrid" work environment is here to stay. And it's not just adults feeling the effects. Children do as well. School is normally the center of their lives. Yet they're staying at home for online education as school districts continue to adjust to outbreaks. Working alone, looking at faces on a computer screen. Or working alongside a brother or sister. It's an adaptation that decreases and/or removes social interaction.

Two of our family friends took their lives this year—people who never displayed any such inclination during their lives. Though they didn't know each other, they shared a common trait; they were very social people who became isolated. Did their isolation contribute to their condition? What I do know is that social interaction is important to health maintenance at all ages.

In a recent article published by the National Institutes of Health entitled Social Wellness Toolkit, the NIH cites six strategies for improving your social health:

- Take care of yourself while caring for others
- Get active together
- Bond with your kids
- Build healthy relationships
- Shape your family's health habits
- Make connections

As you read these strategies, you may find, as I did, that the author assumes you will be maintaining social contacts, i.e., getting out of the house and mingling. You will see in the attached picture how I stay connected, in this example, with my family. The challenge is to avoid allowing fear of the virus to isolate us from our family, friends, and colleagues.

Social interaction is critical to family life, career success, and overall health and wellbeing. It's time to get out and enjoy.

*Statistical data is collected from multiple sources that update at various times and may not always align. Some locations may provide incomplete information.

Chapter 17

Blood Test Detects 50 Cancer Types
March 17, 2024

Many people have well-established relationships with physicians in a variety of medical specialties. One of the values of regular visits to these specialists is cancer detection. Each specialist in their own way is a primary identification point for certain types of cancer. In the aggregate, today, they form the intermediary for early detection.

On June 25, 2021, NHS England, which oversees the National Health Service in England, announced it is rolling out a pilot of a simple blood screening test which, it states, can "...detect more than 50 types of cancer before any clinical signs or symptoms of the disease emerge in a person...' including '...many types of the disease that are difficult to diagnose in the early stages such as head and neck, ovarian, pancreatic, esophageal, and some blood cancers." The article describes very promising results from an initial test of more than twenty-eight hundred subjects.

The blood test was developed by Grail, a U.S.-based company, where Dr. Eric Klein, Glickman Urological and Kidney Institute at Cleveland Clinic Chair, was first author on the research. In Dr. Klein's words, "These data suggest that, if used alongside existing screening tests, the multi-cancer detection test could have a profound impact on how cancer is detected and, ultimately, on public health." It has long been recognized that early diagnosis leads to more successful treatment.

No mention is made in the article as to the expected cost of such testing should it become available. It is understood that the matter of coverage by insurance companies is critical as well. Imagine the clinical advantage to those people receiving an early cancer diagnosis whose disease would otherwise remain undetected with potential for metastasis.

It will be vital to the long-term success of this diagnostic tool to achieve successful clinical trials, quick approval by regulators, low final unit cost of testing, and financial reward to the test developers.

Business Matters

Chapter 18

Applying Business Practices to Family Risk Management

December 31, 2023

Profitability is the primary goal of a business. If a company's product has a sustainable competitive advantage, and the market is willing to pay the asking price for that product, there is no reason for the company not to be profitable. But there are systemic risks to profitability that go beyond product-market fit, and most successful enterprises—certainly larger ones—carefully monitor and manage those risks.

One profitable, growing health insurance company, with which I am familiar, has identified the following high-level risks to its ongoing success.

1. Breach of data integrity
2. Ongoing reduction in new sales
3. Loss of existing customers
4. Failure to retain good business partners
5. Investment losses and reduced investment income
6. Unsustainable increases in claims and/or expenses
7. Legal actions

The company views these risks (though not an exhaustive list) as the most significant influences on its profitability. Note: these are not anecdotal or one-off risks (e.g., quoted premium to a customer is calculated in error, a customer phone call gets dropped, or a request-for-proposal from a salesperson gets ignored). Those kinds of routine errors, while aggravating, are typically managed in the course of business by supervisors and middle managers. However, the high-level risks are serious enough to cause material loss—even threatening the solvency of the business. They are the responsibility of the most senior executives.

"So what?" you ask. "What does this health insurance company have to do with me, and why is it important?" The purpose of this paper is not to analyze the list of risks to this company nor how the company should best address them. That's the role of their executives. But the threats posed to this company are no different than the threats posed to individuals. Families face the same risk challenges as a business enterprise. They are the same risks in another form.

Consider asking, "How can I learn from this model to manage the risks to my and my family's financial wellbeing?"

Let's look at the high-level risks this company identified and then apply them to a typical family. What specific threats to its wellness must the family address? What should the family's "senior executives" be concerned about? Below are a few examples.

1. Breach of data integrity

    a. Predictable and unprotected passwords
    b. Identity theft
    c. Excessive and overly revealing participation on social media
    d. Falling for scams

2. Ongoing reduction in new sales and loss of existing customers (for individuals, this means loss of sources of income)

    a. Less than expected bonus
    b. Less than expected raise
    c. Laid off from job
    d. Sickness, disability, or death

3. Failure to retain good business partners

    a. Deteriorating relationship with your boss
    b. Failure to continually develop new business contacts
    c. Failure to establish and maintain a formal network program
    d. Failure to identify and pursue employment alternatives

4. Investment losses and reduced investment income

    a. Attempting to "time the market"
    b. Unnecessarily risky investments for your circumstances
    c. Losses greater than "market losses"
    d. Failure to make savings, retirement, and investment plan contributions

5. Unsustainable increases in claims and/or expenses

    a. Lack of family budget
    b. Expenses exceed available income
    c. Using home equity loan for something other than home improvement or debt consolidation (e.g., vacation, new boat)

6. Legal actions

    a. Engage in activity which could result in a lawsuit (e.g., assault your neighbor during an argument, run over your neighbor's dog backing out of your driveway too fast)
    b. Ignore sources of personal negligence (e.g., swimming pool unfenced, tree overhanging neighbor's property, pool of oil where the mail carrier delivers your mail, dog uncontrolled)
    c. Routinely drive in an unsafe manner
    d. Fail to meet contractual obligations
    e. Fail to meet regulatory requirements (e.g., don't show up for jury duty, forget to renew personal or business licenses)

This is not a "how to" list. There's nothing new in these examples. But have you addressed them? Consider the following.

1. Expand the list. Identify and understand your high-level risks
2. Prioritize those risks
3. Assign accountability for management of risks (self, spouse, children, third parties)
4. Mitigate risks and take corrective action
5. Implement your list. At minimum, include these action items:

    a. Protect your identity and personal information
    b. Make yourself indispensable at work
    c. Establish high quality physician relationships and see them regularly
    d. Buy health insurance—even if in great health
    e. Network, network, network

f. Ask your insurance agent for a comprehensive risk assessment

g. Obtain help with investment management

h. Buy liability insurance—especially a high-limit umbrella policy

i. Analyze and manage insurance deductibles and policy limits wisely

j. Acquaint yourself with an attorney so one is available in an emergency

k. Put your plan in writing

When you have completed this process, you'll have a wellness plan for managing your risk just like Microsoft and Apple—though yours can be implemented more quickly. We can't eliminate all risk, but your family enterprise can take comfort that you are employing sound business practices, and you will have done your best to mitigate its financial risk.

Chapter 19

Virtual Insurance Company
November 1, 2021

For years, decentralization and outsourcing—often internationally—worked well for companies manufacturing a product. Those companies sought any means to maximize efficiency and reduce costs. Manufacturing jobs moved out of the US to lower-cost countries. Everything was less expensive—raw materials, component parts, manufacturing, sub-assembly, shipping, and final assembly. In this country, shipping, warehousing, and final delivery to the customer were subcontracted. And it all worked—until it didn't. The virus came. Then, if one step was interrupted, the entire process shut down.

A capacity shortage at any point can break the chain and create an interruption. In March 2020, there was no hand sanitizer on the shelves. Not because there was no hand sanitizer but because a change in demand occurred. People who had never heard of hand sanitizer now wanted four bottles. How overwhelming for the subcontractors supplying hand sanitizer. The chain, beginning with the sourcing of the raw materials for hand sanitizer and ending with the retail grocery stores, broke.

How did the United States find itself with China as the sole importer of face masks? Because, before the virus, China was the cheapest manufacturer. Therefore, we imported from China. But, with the supply chain interrupted, when China shut down because of the virus, they needed the masks and had none for export.

U.S. Manufacturing has begun to rethink the outsourcing of stages of production—particularly in high-precision, high-tech products. It may be time to bring the supply chain back home. It is happening with chipmakers.

But what about financial services companies such as insurance companies and asset managers? What have they been doing to outsource and subcontract functions? Health insurance companies have outsourced claims functions to other, lower-cost countries for years. First Ireland, then India and now the Philippines. But beyond that?

Most insurance companies have geographically diversified functions. For example, sales offices are typically scattered across the companies' service areas. Claims and policyholder services are housed in lower-cost regions. Financial, regulatory, and planning functions are normally in the home office. In each of those locations, a staff of specialists, organized in a traditional management hierarchy, does the work.

Companies are structured like Meridian Life and Health Insurance Company (a hypothetical traditional company I will use as an example). Vice presidents and directors oversee a staff of managers and specialists doing specific jobs such as those in the following organization chart.

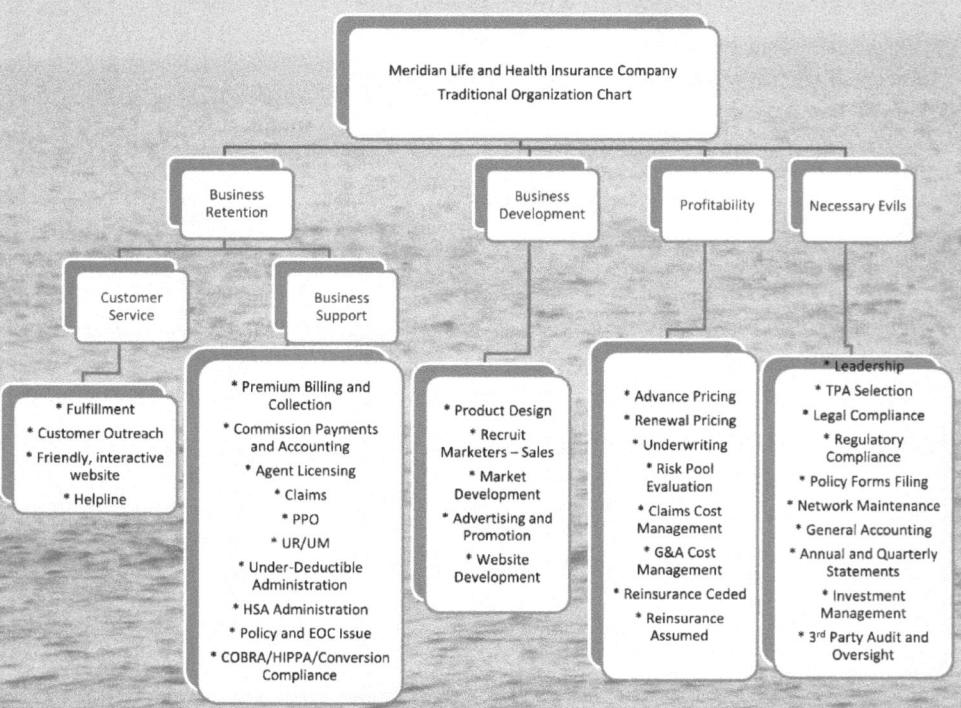

But financial services companies are different from manufacturing companies. There are no raw materials to become scarce. There is no sub-assembly to be disrupted by a virus outbreak. There are no warehouses to confiscate by a foreign government. There is no assembly line for a union to shut down. There are no delivery services to be overwhelmed by a surge in demand. Every function within a financial services company can be performed anywhere.

Today, over half of American workers report working from home at least part time, the percentage being higher for traditional white-collar workers. One result of this transition has been to validate the concept that businesses can function efficiently with a workforce in remote locations. This is especially true of knowledge workers and those who work primarily at a computer—such as in an insurance company.

When the pandemic hit, one health insurance company in southern California converted from a two-location company with all employees on site to 100 percent remote in only 3 days—reportedly with no loss of productivity and efficiency. Hundreds of other businesses have reported comparable results and high levels of employee satisfaction. In companies which survey their employees, most find that employees would gladly continue to work remotely as businesses reopen. When combined with the trend toward outsourcing functions, a compelling case can be made for a financial services company to transition to a virtual model.

What does this mean for a hypothetical company like Meridian Life and Health Insurance Company? Here is the plan Meridian Life could be contemplating.

The Meridian Life and Health Insurance Company Virtual Model

Every insurance company chief executive officer in America strives to make his/her company more efficient—eliminating unnecessary layers of cost and achieving continuous improvement in the quality and profitability of the company's products and services. The virtual insurance company does just that. It functions without employees. At the extreme, the company will contract out every function to a "Best-of Class" subcontractor and leave no one in the company except the CEO who does the contracting and manages the relationships.

The Meridian Virtual Model, specifically designed for a small or medium size insurance company, approaches that goal. There are only five employees in this company—three executives, an accountant/actuary and an enterprising, industrious protégé. The clever CEO will be on the lookout for an opportunity to give a generous separation bonus to one of the other two executives and roll that person's functions up into a new contracted relationship.

Meridian Life will be unique in America. The industry and the larger business community will read with interest about Meridian Life and marvel at the brilliance and simplicity of the concept. Warren Buffett will want to meet the CEO because this is how Buffett runs his enterprise; he has only fifteen employees in the home office of his company which employs over 350,000 people.

The basic premise of the Meridian Life Virtual Model is that every insurance company can contract out every function to a third party. The costs of the services contracted for are less than the costs at the company can provide those services on its own. Meridian Life will reduce general and administrative expenses by over 20 percent in the first operational year and by upwards of 30 percent in subsequent years—creating enormous competitive pricing advantage.

In addition to reducing costs, the company will dramatically improve every aspect of the customer experience. Today, Managing General Agents specialize in product distribution. TPAs specialize in the support functions of policy issue, risk-selection, billing, claims, and customer service. Actuarial consultants set rates, establish reserves, and prepare financial statements. Legal and compliance consultants file policies and assure regulatory compliance. It is their business to be at the forefront. Meridian Life will engage the "Best of Class." Every such expert vendor will provide services superior to that which Meridian Life can provide on its own. No longer will Meridian Life invest in "systems" which are inefficient, labor-intensive, and quickly out-of-date.

Technological advances such as using avatars and other virtual reality will be differentiating points among the various third-party vendors. Those which continue to develop and evolve innovative technology will gain and retain relationships with Meridian.

There is no supply chain. Every function is performed independently of the others. None relies on another. Except for executive involvement in the War Room (proprietary data center), no staff is required on the company site. No time is spent managing employees. The facility will need only about 3,000 square feet.

As in all successful implementations, there are critical success factors for the Meridian Life Virtual Model. They are:

a. complete and absolute buy-in by the five employees,
b. establishing clear, precise expectations of the contractors,
c. holding the contractors strictly accountable for performance and
d. creation and monitoring of the "War Room"

The five employees will ensure that all required functions are performed expertly. The primary roles of the three executives are to identify and engage the "Best-of-Class" service providers, relentlessly manage the relationships, and create and monitor the War Room. They will spend their time on site visits, reviewing vendor proposals, and unceasingly monitoring performance metrics.

From the day a decision is made to implement the Meridian Virtual Model in an existing company, the full implementation process will require fifteen months.

(Employee descriptions and accountabilities, relationship management assignments, war room description, implementation schedule and cost estimates, are available upon request.)

Chapter 20

Back to Service Basics

October 1, 2021

When I grew up, I often rode with my father while he met with clients for Wyandotte Chemicals Corporation. Through this experience, I learned what effective customer service means.

My father developed relationships with his clients and regularly treated them to a meal or snack while discussing business. He always responded to phone or written inquiries without delay, even late at night. As I tagged along, I remember thinking that every client must surely appreciate the attentiveness he gave them, the success they achieved with his products, and the trust they developed in his faithful service.

As a registered nurse, I originally graduated from a three-year hospital program, the gold standard for clinical training at that time. Abbott Northwestern required nurses to have effective communication by employing active listening with patients. I continued to published practice the service standards I learned years ago.

Why should this not be today's standard? Not just within the medical profession but with all businesses?

During my healthcare and business career, I expected that businesses would be dependable, answer the phone, or return communications and have incentive to effectively provide customer service to me as a customer. For years in the Midwest, this is exactly the experience I had.

However, during the past fifteen years on the West Coast, I've had to change my expectations. My phone and email requests frequently go unanswered. My father's service level is simply nonexistent, and businesses are often not open during their business hours.

Is it because the times are changing or does West Coast culture differ from the Midwest in business practice? The complexity of modern business is not a valid excuse. Simply because employees receive 150 emails, voicemails, or texts every day does not relieve the company of its service responsibility.

Effective communication is almost universally cited as a business goal. That initiative often means better communication with employees. Less often, it means better communication with customers. When I'm spending money on a product or service, I want an efficient, personalized resolution or a way to resolve the problem promptly. I hope the company will begin the interaction with the foregone conclusion that they will agree to my request (not search for a reason to deny it). Large companies like Costco, Nordstrom, Apple, and Amazon understand this and flourish—even in the face of great competition. Others may not.

Innovative products and services are great, but companies must put customer service at the same level of importance. Customer service is not the department to place every entry-level employee. Those who are employed must be trained and managed with the same thoroughness as any other discipline within the company. Those not suited for the role should be freed to work for the competition. Finally, the company should seriously consider a Customer Relationship Management program to assure company-wide attention to customer service and to provide leadership with the means to track and manage performance.

Chapter 21

The Importance of Pricing Power
January 28, 2021

A not-so-familiar name to the general population is back in the spotlight this week. Chamath Palihapitiya, a multi-billionaire investor, has been very vocal about the recent extreme volatility in certain otherwise lackluster-performing stocks (GameStop, AMC, Bed Bath and Beyond, ...). But he is better known for his insight into valuing companies—especially not-so-well-known companies.

Palihapitiya, who lifted himself out of abject poverty in Sri Lanka to become one of Silicon Valley's most respected investors (after being a key executive at Facebook/Meta), came to my attention when I first heard him discuss what he considers to be one of the most important qualities he looks for in making an investment - what he calls the product/market fit.

Palihapitiya recently commented on CNBC:

> A company must understand the product/market fit. The successful company is selling a product that someone wants to buy, who is willing to pay the company's price for it, and the market is sufficiently large to support the business. As an investor, you need to be especially careful when you do not, fundamentally, have a product that is compelling enough to win customers naturally.....and that the only way you can overcome the reluctance of customers to buy your product is through the brute force use of money (price reductions, higher commissions, more incentives, increased marketing, etc.).

Interestingly, a better-known multi-billionaire investor, Warren Buffett, has been quoted as saying something similar although with more simplicity:

> The single most weighty decision in evaluating a business is pricing power. If you have the power to raise prices without losing business to a competitor, you have a particularly good business. If you have a prayer session before you raise your prices by 10 percent, you've got a terrible business.

It's not surprising, then, that companies like Starbucks, Microsoft, Netflix, and Apple, to name just a few, are favored investments. Customers want their products, they will pay what is charged, and the markets for the products are huge. They have an excellent product/market fit. I suspect that experts as diverse as Chamath Palihapitiya and Warren Buffett would agree.

Chapter 22

Your Health is an Investment—Until it Becomes an Expense
February 27, 2023

Preparing and eating healthy meals, expending energy to exercise, and maintaining relationships with a broad range of healthcare professionals, are essential investments in good health. Healthy diet and exercise are linked to increased life expectancy. And health plans long ago proved how active preventive healthcare is associated with disease prevention.

But, if you don't make the investment, illness or injury risk increases. Your health may require intervention. And treatment can quickly turn into an expense—sometimes a great expense. Ignore these facts at your peril.

Consider the cost of health insurance. Do you really know the cost? It is typical to be aware of the amount taken from our paychecks. But what if you leave your job (as fifteen percent of us do every year)? You're on your own then. According to KKK Employee Benefits Survey 2021, your family's health insurance will cost more than twenty thousand dollars annually. And that's just the beginning. There are still deductibles, co-pays, and uninsured expenses to consider.

Why does health insurance cost so much—especially when more individuals are in good health than poor health? Because of those individuals who are not in good health when claims costs are pooled. Those in poorer health raise the cost for the rest of us. Of the twenty thousand dollars annual family health insurance cost, around seventeen thousand dollars (the 85 percent medical loss ratio) goes for the cost of care. On average, over six thousand dollars for hospital bills, four thousand dollars for physicians and clinics, and seven thousand dollars for everything else (according to the CDC).

How can that be, you ask? No one in your family has been in the hospital in years, and you don't spend anywhere near that much on doctors. You eat well, you exercise, and you practice preventive care. But here's the catch—others incur substantial expenses, and you're paying for them. It's not insurance company profits that cause increased costs, it's the people in poor health.

Why should you pay for them? Because that's how healthcare economics and insurance work. You're in the same risk pool as the others who are in poor health. You're subsidizing them. Want to beat the system? Get out of the pool with bad risks and into the pool with people like you who eat well, exercise regularly, and practice preventive care.

Find a plan with as high a deductible as you can. Won't you pay more out of pocket than you are accustomed to? Of course. But you will save so much in premiums that your total cost should drop. And you'll still be insured for the catastrophe. And this works whether you pay for your own insurance or get it at work.

That's how professional risk managers assess and finance risk. They pay as low a premium as possible and lower their total costs by carefully managing risk. You already manage the risk by eating well, exercising, and seeking preventive care. Now, lower your premium as well.

Do yourself a favor. Approach healthcare expenses like a business executive. Manage the risk, and keep expenses at a minimum. Your health will improve, and your wallet will be fatter.

Chapter 23

Medical Expenses Not Covered by Insurance
November 1, 2021

Health care is expensive enough. Have you ever been surprised by a medical bill which was not covered by insurance? Or your employer does not provide dental insurance, and you are facing the expense of three crown replacements? Is there anything you can do?

There is quite a bit you can do. First, look at your recent health insurance benefit statements. The following is an example:

- Cardiologist bill - $387. Insurance paid $192. No balance due. Fifty percent paid.
- Cardiologist bill - $139. Insurance paid $47. No balance due. Thirty-four percent paid.
- Surgeon bill - $1,850. Insurance paid $725. No balance due. Thirty-nine percent paid.
- Hospital Outpatient Surgery bill - $12,575. Insurance paid $2,356. No balance due. Nineteen percent paid.

If providers will accept less than half their billed amounts from the insurance companies, why should you have to pay their billed amount just because the expense is not covered by insurance? The answer is you do not.

Have you ever asked a Macy's sales clerk to accept a price lower than the marked price on an item? I remember an instructor in a managerial accounting class who recommended we consider asking for a discount at retail stores. And it works for healthcare providers too.

A patient recently needed physical therapy, but the preferred clinic was not contracted with his insurance company. He requested that the office manager charge him exactly what they would receive from a Blue Cross patient. It was around fifty-five percent of what they were going to otherwise charge. They accepted his offer, and he continued receiving care from them. The same can be negotiated with a dental clinic. For example, if their reimbursements are around sixty percent of what they normally charge an uninsured patient, this becomes a business proposition. Make an appointment and discuss it with the practice manager, not front desk staff. Discounts are there for the asking.

All of this assumes you have not received the service yet. But what if you have already received treatment and are facing an unexpectedly large bill? There are companies which negotiate discounted payments on large non-contracted bills on behalf of insurance companies every day. Those companies are often successful in negotiating discounts upwards of eighty percent of the bills they negotiate with savings approaching fifty percent. How do they do it? They ask.

They know reimbursement is often delayed. Armed with that knowledge, they offer to pay, say, sixty five percent of the bill that same day if the provider will accept it as payment in full. Frequently, the answer will be yes. The providers want the money, and today is preferred.

You can do it too. Explain that because of the high amount of the bill, you will have to pay it off over several months or more. Alternatively, you could get them a check today (for ~ fifty percent) in exchange for release of liability for the balance. It might work, and it will surely allow you some discount on the balance you owe.

If you happen to be insured by Medicare, you have another protection. Medicare requires physicians to provide you with a written Advance Beneficiary Notice (ABN) in the event the treating physician has any reason to expect that a normally covered service might be denied by Medicare. This allows you to decide whether to receive the service. The ABN is to include the nature of the services which might be denied as well as the cost of those services.

Frequently, providers do not provide such a notice or ABN but bill for the service anyway. In cases where a patient is not provided with an ABN, the patient may not be billed by the provider when Medicare denies payment.

If this happens to you and you are billed, let the provider know they did not provide the required notice.

Be a good consumer of healthcare just as you are when you negotiate the price of a new car. Savings are available, sometimes substantial savings, if you ask for them.

Chapter 24

Should You Care About Insurance Fraud?

July 14, 2023

During my business career in managed healthcare, I frequently took part in discussions about the potential effect of fraud on a business proposition. "If we implement this plan," so the question went, "do we open ourselves up to fraud?" Recent reports of Medicare fraud caused me to give serious thought to the extent to which fraud impacts insurance cost and a family's budget.

The insurance industry in the United States collects over $1.3 trillion in premiums annually. Approximately 60 percent of this premium goes to life insurance, health insurance and annuity companies. The remaining 40 percent goes to property/casualty insurers.

How much is $1.3 trillion? Well, it's three times the total amount of all corporate income taxes paid to the federal government in the United States. It's about equal to the entire economy of Australia. In short, it's a considerable amount of money.

But why worry about fraud? Those rich insurance companies can afford it. Right? They collect and collect, but they never pay out. Or so the complaint goes. It's their problem, not mine.

So why is the size of the U.S. insurance industry important? Because a great deal of that money is fraudulently misdirected through criminal enterprise. How much? Below is information assembled by the Coalition Against Insurance Fraud.

- Insurance fraud steals at least $80 billion every year from American consumers. (Coalition Against Insurance Fraud is working to update this figure in 2022).
- Fraud occurs in about 10 percent of property-casualty insurance losses (Insurance Information Institute, 2017, "Insurance Fraud").
- Medicare fraud is estimated to cost $60 billion every year (AARP 2018).

A billion here, a billion there, soon we're talking serious money. And it does affect the individual. The FBI estimates that every American household pays between $400 and $700 extra per year because of insurance fraud—and this excludes health insurance fraud! Does that get your attention?

So, how does insurance fraud take place? Below are examples of common ways. Your companies may have experienced this firsthand.

- Application fraud. It starts with the applicant who lies on an application for insurance. Any willful misrepresentation of health or business status on an application is a crime. And it happens every day – by both applicants and their agents (sometimes without the applicant's knowledge). People and businesses who are otherwise uninsurable obtain insurance illegally.
- Claims fraud by the insured. Most common are false claims by insureds for benefits. People report a theft that never took place. People fake disability to receive monthly benefits. They even fake death. Or, as in a famous crime during the 1990s, they kill show horses who have become insured for more than their value. They set fires to property or exaggerate claims for worthless assets. And worse. They take the life of another person to collect life insurance.
- And it's not limited to insured parties. Hospitals, physicians, and dentists have been known to overinflate the cost of services they perform. The largest Medicare fraud case in U.S. history settled against a hospital group for inflated claims. Every day, we read about a lab billing Medicare for tests they never performed or a doctor billing patients he or she never treated.
- Agents and third-party administrators are potentially able to do the most fraud damage. Frequently, they manage insurance company money – premiums collected from clients, and in certain cases, the funds used to pay claims. It can be tempting for an agent or administrator to divert premium to their own account and never remit

it to the insurance company. And if an administrator is also contracted to pay claims on behalf of the insurance company, the opportunity to misdirect claim funds to illegal ends can be powerful. Fake claims here and there can quickly add up to fund an elaborate lifestyle.

- Auditor collusion. Read about Enron and Arthur Andersen. Though not an insurance company, what happened in the Enron case might just as well happen to an insurance company. Imagine trusting your business insurance to a company whose balance sheet was fraudulently maintained. What if, at the time of your devastating loss, the insurance company was insolvent and unable to pay because of fraud? This is less common today than fifty years ago, but it still is possible.

Insurance fraud is everyone's problem. It's not just "rich" insurance companies who suffer. It's you and me who pay higher premiums to subsidize fake claims and theft. You may never have your premium stolen by an agent, be the victim of a contrived auto accident, or be "insured" by a non-existent company. But you are paying for it.

Chapter 25

A Challenge for Leadership
May 21, 2021

The basic pros and cons of returning to the office after working remotely differ for the employee and the employer. Working in the office improves communications, reduces work distractions, adds additional technology, and provides necessary social interaction. On the other hand, an employee returning to the office incurs commuting stress and expense, requires a reevaluation of time management, and may introduce health risks.

But what about the longer-term view? What will work look like in the future, and how do we plan for it now? Will we work remotely three days a week and on-site two days a week, or will we simply work five days a week in the most efficient way with no reference to on-site or off-site?

In an interview on CNBC, Microsoft CEO Satya Nadella commented on what he calls "hybrid work." He stated that the new reality of work will require adjustment of people, place, and process in many ways.

Not all CEOs are aligned as to how to proceed. Some want everyone back in the office. Some believe that complete flexibility—even one hundred percent remote work—is preferred. Of course, frequently, it depends on the business. But flexibility seems to be the key—for both employers and employees. Both should be ready to accommodate new realities and make the necessary adjustments.

According to many surveys, an overwhelming percentage of employees enjoy the comfort and convenience of working from home and don't want to return to the office. Not surprisingly, the Microsoft survey revealed that seventy-three percent of its employees want work flexibility. Among the same group, however, sixty-seven percent also said, somewhat paradoxically, they want more personal interaction with others.

Yet another executive has reported results differently. Sandeep Mathrani, CEO of WeWork, stated in The Wall Street Journal's Future of Everything Festival, "Those who are uberly engaged with the company want to go to the office two-thirds of the time, at least. Those who are least engaged are very comfortable working from home."

Business leaders will be required to add management of this condition to their already formidable list of challenges. Are companies saving money? Are people more satisfied? Will hiring managers require upgraded qualifications when people aren't in person to train? It could occupy them for years.

Chapter 26

The Future for Long Term Care Insurance

June 16, 2023

Are you familiar with Long-Term Care Insurance (LTCI)? I suspect that you are in that it's been around for almost forty years. Do you own an LTCI policy? Probably not. It would seem like a "no-brainer" to buy a LTCI policy. We all know someone in a senior living setting or who is receiving home care. And we know long-term care isn't inexpensive. But according to The American Association for Long Term Care Insurance only about eight million people under 65 currently have such coverage. Why so few?

The main reason people don't buy LTCI is cost since people simply may not be able to afford it. If they were fortunate enough to work for an employer who sponsored an LTCI plan, and they enrolled in their fifties, the premiums might be affordable. But if they wait until they reach age sixty-five, a policy is often unaffordable. In 2021, only eleven percent of all buyers of LTCI were over sixty-five. And it's not just cost. By waiting to enroll until after age sixty-five, health becomes a significant factor. Almost forty percent of applicants over sixty-five are declined for health reasons. The insurers don't want to cover them.

But there's another reason for low enrollment. People may not need LTCI. They or their families have sufficient resources, and not every contingency has to be insured. So, the market for this insurance is even narrower. People below a certain income threshold can't afford it. Those above a higher threshold don't need it. The narrow band in between is the market. And 40 percent of them get rejected.

The LTCI insurers appear capable. But few are successfully making money. In fact, G.E. Capital was under-reserved by over fifteen billion dollars because of LTCI and effectively put out of the LTCI business. Once the largest corporation in the world, General Electric, its owner, is now an afterthought in large measure because of the collapse of its LTCI business.

Even today, insurers frequently require premium increase on existing policyholders. Of course, they must get approval from state insurance commissioners, but they still face pricing quandaries. The companies have done a poor job of assessing risk, and when risk goes up, the price to insure it soon follows. And the policyholders are stuck. They feel they have paid years of premiums and can't afford not to keep the insurance in force. Only five percent allow their coverage to lapse each year—and in most cases it's because the policyholder passes away.

So, where does that leave us? Potential buyers won't buy the product and insurers don't make money on the product. The answer is setting money aside for personal and family savings, just as with funding for retirement, a home, or a car. People set money aside to purchase or finance large expenses. Long term care is no different. It's time to realize that LTCI is not a practical solution for most people.

Do certain people need help paying for care? Of course. But this is a societal problem, not an insurance problem. One size does not fit all. Should there be a safety net such as with Social Security? Maybe. A means-tested allowance? We'll see. But despite what the insurers tell us, long-term care insurance will not become one of the foundations of family financial planning

Chapter 27

Health Insurance For International Travel
February 10, 2022

Have you finally had enough of Covid? Do the rivers of Europe beckon? Have you always wanted to visit the South Pacific? Are you so ready to go off to those places you were going to visit two years ago? You're not alone.

Before you leave, however, there's one more important matter to take care of: health insurance. That's right, our old favorite. We may be tired of the topic but it's critical that anyone planning to leave the country take a careful look at health insurance and make the appropriate plans. You do not want to require emergency surgery in a foreign country and be responsible for the costs of a lengthy hospitalization and doctors' charges.

Broadly, there are three groups: those covered by Medicare, those covered by other insurance such as through their employment, and those who are not covered at all.

If you are covered by traditional Medicare and have purchased a supplement, you may have some coverage. It is likely to be an 80 percent reimbursement after a $250 deductible. The maximum benefit is $50,000. Sounds OK. But, $50,000 won't go too far in case of a serious emergency and it is a lifetime maximum, not per year or per trip. And if you haven't purchased a supplement, you are unlikely to have coverage. Do you have a Medicare Advantage plan? You may have a travel supplement added on or you may not. It is up to your insurer. You must ask them before you go.

If you are covered by a traditional health insurance policy, such as through your employer or through an insurance exchange, you will have to consult the policy details. Some will cover foreign travel, at least on a limited basis, but many do not. Of course, if you have no health insurance in the U.S., you won't be covered outside the country.

What should you do about it? First, be certain you know what coverage you do have. Call the company that insures you. Ask all the questions. See it in writing.

After you know your coverage, or lack thereof, you may need to fill in the gap. If so, give serious consideration to an international travel insurance policy. A quick search of the Internet will reveal a lengthy list of qualified insurers. The cost for a trip of a few weeks is reasonable—or, at least worth the peace of mind. And be sure to ask if medical evacuation is covered. While it is unlikely that you will ever need to be flown by air ambulance back to the United States, it could happen. And the cost can be considerable.

Be careful of what is called 'travel insurance" as opposed to "international travel health insurance." They are not the same. The former may sound comprehensive but not cover your emergency health care needs. And remember, if you do incur health care expenses while traveling outside the U.S., you will be required to pay for them on the spot. You will then have to submit your paid bills to your insurer for reimbursement. (A few travel health insurers do have international PPOs which will accept your insurance as payment. Few do, however.)

Bon Voyage!

Chapter 28

Billionaires and the American Dream
April 25, 2023

I thought about the American Dream this week—the notion that our society provides the platform for personal success and upward mobility through hard work—independent of royal lineage or caste. I believe in the American Dream. But then, I wondered, is it different for billionaires? Whatever billionaires are, they're not like me. And it's not just the money, although that has a great deal to do with it. They're simply different. How? The following are examples.

Elon Musk's company SpaceX launched the most powerful rocket ever made. Four minutes into the flight, it exploded. He and his company celebrated the event. Celebrated what most would consider a failure.

Then I remembered September 2008, near the worst point in the great financial crisis. Warren Buffett invested five billion in Goldman Sachs, which desperately needed capital. He put his money at risk when the entire world economy teetered on the brink of collapse.

Jeff Bezos enjoyed an extraordinarily successful early career in financial technology. Then, though well paid, and despite the enormous competition from freestanding bookstores like Barnes and Noble, Borders, Crown, and Waldenbooks, he risked all his money. Working from his garage, he formed an online bookseller, Amazon.

When seeing a major investment explode, it would be typical to experience enormous grief, not joy. Or, if the world financial system faced disaster, one would put whatever cash and investable assets owned into U.S. Treasury Bills, not in a high-risk business. Or, if employed in a high-paying job in a fast-growing industry, one would consider themselves fortunate and invest their earnings wisely, not risk it all in an unproven venture. At least, that's what I'd do.

Yet, these three men saw things differently. Musk, Buffett, and Bezos each envisioned success despite failure or the potential for failure. They assumed risks others would shun. A contemporary of theirs, Bill Gates, took the risk of dropping out of Harvard without a degree to chase his dream.

In addition to great wealth, these men share other qualities. They are willing to take risks. But what makes them different from the guy at the racetrack is that they know how to quantify, limit, and reduce risk because they understand it. They are optimistic for good reasons. They see opportunities where others don't and have a keen instinct for identifying when they have an advantage that's worth the risk.

Another common thread is an enterprising spirit—a relentless work ethic and a single-mindedness to succeed. And they all started to think like entrepreneurs early in life. Warren Buffett washed cars, delivered newspapers, and sold door-to-door to raise money to invest. He started trading stocks at age eleven. He always knew he wanted to be an investor. His company, Berkshire Hathaway, is one of the ten largest companies, by market capitalization, in the United States.

Even before he graduated from high school, Jeff Bezos began formulating ideas of when men would colonize space. He never stopped. Today, in addition to being Chair of Amazon, he is the founder of Blue Origin, a competitor of Musk's SpaceX. Amazon is also one of the ten largest companies in the United States.

Bill Gates began programming at age thirteen and has been doing so ever since. At eighteen, he developed a programming algorithm to solve what mathematicians called an "unsolvable problem," and at age twenty, founded what became Microsoft. Microsoft is now the second largest company in the United States.

All three stayed with and earned their fortunes through their basic brand. Buffett the investor, Bezos the engineer, and Gates the programmer. Only Musk parlayed early success into diversified businesses, evolving the sale of a game at age twelve into Zip2 at age twenty-four, then to PayPal, to

Tesla, to SpaceX, and, finally, Twitter (X) at age fifty-one (with numerous other ventures thrown in to keep him busy). Tesla, where he is chairman of the board, is now one of the largest companies in the United States.

What are these men best known for—besides their wealth? All believe in taking quantifiable and measured risk. All believe in themselves and are willing to invest everything they own in their ideas—their wealth comes from their own companies. And all have a single-mindedness to succeed and will accept nothing less.

By contrast, I worked my way through school, became a nurse, raised children, and pursued a second career in managed healthcare. Though I believed in myself and worked hard, I fell short of my own expectations. On those occasions, I didn't always recognize the value of setbacks. Maybe that's why I'm not a billionaire.

Chapter 29

Hybrid Work

May 4, 2021

Americans just completed the Memorial Day weekend, the unofficial start of summer. Although we celebrate Memorial Day to remember and mourn the deaths of military personnel who died serving our country, it is also the first extended getaway weekend of the year. Three or four days that can be spent enjoying family and non-work pleasures.

This year, it's also a reminder. The grip of the pandemic is easing, and millions of Americans who have been working from home now face a return to some form of office environment. After a year of forced confinement, many are recognizing the need for a healthy balance between work and leisure. And the reopening of business is the perfect time to do something about it.

It has not taken long for "Hybrid Work" to move to a position of prominence in the lexicon of overworked business buzzwords. Companies are fashioning plans to determine the best balance of on-site and remote work. A May 04, 2021, article from the Harvard Business Review entitled "What Mix of WFH and Office Time Is Right for You?" by Robert C. Pozen and Alexandra Samuel, describes how some calculate the balance. What better time for you to take part in the calculation.

Employers are examining every work process as our economy reopens. They need the input of everyone, not just the creator of "Hybrid Work." The new paradigm must also recognize the health benefits of work-life balance. Will your company's hybrid work plan address your health?

One thing is certain. You must take the initiative. We all benefit from recognizing the value of work-life balance and doing something about it. If you do not, no one else will. Not your company, not your boss, not the other commuters on the freeway, not the other demands of your life.

You do not have to wait until the 4th of July to enjoy work-life balance.

Chapter 30

Monte Carlo
July 14, 2023

What is Monte Carlo best known for? You might say something like, "A city on the French Riviera known for its luxurious lifestyle, international clientele, and renowned casino. It is a destination for the world's rich and famous." And you would be right. Monte Carlo is all those things.

But it is also the name given to a mathematical technique used to estimate outcomes of an uncertain event. The Monte Carlo simulation. It gains its name from the fact that it utilizes random samples, not unlike the random results which occur at the gaming tables in Monte Carlo.

Here's an example. Suppose you were interested in knowing the likelihood of exactly two heads and four tails appearing if you dropped six coins on a table. It's a simple mathematical calculation. But, if you didn't know the math, you could also drop six coins and record the result. Then do it again. In time, you would have dropped the coins a sufficient number of times to have enough data to reach a conclusion. It would not be a precise conclusion, but it would be sufficient for you to know, with little doubt, that you would expect to see exactly two heads 15/64 of the time or about one out of every four throws.

Or you could run a Monte Carlo simulation on your computer. The simulation would replicate you dropping the coins except it would do so hundreds, even thousands of times in just seconds. It would quickly reach the same conclusion you did by dropping coins.

"So, what," you say. Well, there is one very practical application of a Monte Carlo simulation which you may find useful. It has to do with retirement forecasting. How many of us have asked ourselves, "Will my retirement nest egg last throughout my lifetime?" It's an important question to ask and a perfect question for a Monte Carlo simulation.

You could set up your own simulation. Certain variables will be fixed such as your age, gender, annual expenses, regular income sources and current investment portfolio. Other variables would take additional thought. Expected stock market returns, asset allocation, future interest rates, currency exchange rates, future inflation rate, and your life expectancy to name a few. You would need to make estimates for a wide range of variables.

Setting up and running a simulation of hundreds or even thousands of hypothetical results using your data would yield an answer—the likelihood of your financial resources being adequate to fund the remainder of your life. You would see a range of potential outcomes and the probability of each one occurring. But it would take a great deal of time. Or you could let someone else do the heavy lifting.

Financial services companies often provide free calculators to take the work out of setting up a Monte Carlo simulation. Fifteen minutes is all you need to enter your data and run your simulation. In no time, you will know if you are on the right track.

There is yet another use of the term Monte Carlo. Years ago, I drove a 1974 Monte Carlo. It was so old, the state exempted it from smog check. They considered it a "Classic." But that's another story.

Chapter 31

To Estimate or Not to Estimate; That is the Question

December 21, 2022

Do you usually leave a 15 percent percent tip in the restaurant? When you see your bill for $65.89, do you reach into your pocket, get out your phone, scroll around, and select the app for the calculator, search for the percent sign, enter 15 percent x $65.89, note that the answer is $9.8835 and try to remember, "Do I round up to 89 cents or not?" Is that you?

Or do you instantly see that 10 percent of the bill is around $6.60 and if you add half, that's another $3.30 for a total of $9.90 and put a ten-dollar bill on the table giving the matter no further thought? Is it 15 percent? That depends. If you're teaching a lesson in sixth grade arithmetic, no, it's not. It's a bit higher than 15.1768 percent. But who cares? If you're not a sixth-grade math teacher, yes, it's 15 percent.

Every day, we confront choices of whether to be precise or be right. Being right is different than being precise and can be an improvement. But not always.

I learned lessons early in my career as a nurse. For example, certain decisions between being right and precise are simple. How old is the patient? To make a first evaluation, it's sufficient to note that the patient is "in her eighties." However, when preparing patient identification, an exact birthdate is essential to avoid confusion with other patients.

When I served in a hospital, a physician would at times order a titration of, for example, an ACE Inhibitor or a diuretic. This was common for cardiac patients to determine maximum effective dose while minimizing side effects. It was critical that I measure precise amounts and record all results. There could be no estimating or approximating. If I did not precisely measure the dosage or monitor and record their effects, the physician would be unsure of the results or worse, the patient's life could be at risk. There was no place for estimation.

Is patient body weight important for hospital patient care? Yes, it is measured daily to be aware of condition changes that may require further medical attention. But does it need to be measured precisely? Once again, in my experience, it depends. If a 410-pound candidate is admitted for open heart surgery, it is less critical to know that he weighs 410 pounds. Knowledgably estimating his weight at between 375 and 450 pounds is sufficient to establish that he is morbidly obese, and that the surgery is unlikely to be routine. However, insurance has coverage criteria that expects proper documentation of initial weight. And daily weight measurement is important to confirm fluid and electrolyte status post operatively.

Knowing the precise weight of an unstable, critical patient suffering from renal failure could be lifesaving. A gain or loss of just ounces could be indicative of serious health change. In such cases, I would never rely on estimation.

Later, as I moved into the business side of managed health care, we would analyze customer results. I remember one meeting where a client was presenting the savings it had experienced by implementing one of our programs. In the prior year, they had spent $10,550,000. In the current year, they had reduced their spending to $8,420,000. I recognized that the savings had been around $2,100,000 or around 20 percent of the prior year. Without thinking, I said aloud, "That's great. A 20 percent reduction."

The importance was the magnitude of the savings, not that it was 20.19 percent. Just as important was that others at the table expressed their wonder at how I had made my estimate while they were only then reaching for their calculators. Being able to estimate allowed the conversation to remain on the important topic of cost savings, not precision.

In business, if a sales executive reports that, "Sales this year are up 35 percent," no one cares if it's 33.1 percent or 36.4 percent. It's been a momentous year. It's also true of the source of the sales.

Consider Pareto's Law. During the 19th century, Vilfredo Pareto, an Italian economist, put forward a principle which described the frequency distribution of an empirical relationship of a variate-values pattern. What?

You and I know it better as the 80-20 rule, and every sales executive will tell you that 80 percent of all sales come from 20 percent of the customers. No one cares if it's 81 percent-19 percent. An estimate is fine.

However, if the CFO in the same company publishes an annual statement misstating a single financial detail, the entire statement is called into question, and the company is subject to severe consequences. Regardless of how large the number, if it's wrong by a dollar, it's wrong.

Specialists in healthcare data analytics utilize complex stochastic mathematical modeling to attempt to achieve optimal results in such matters as control of disease transmission through vaccination, appointment scheduling (smoothing out demand), and blood bank stocking (inventory management).

The use of such modeling attempts to optimize a response or policy—to make the best estimate. However, this modeling, though complex, does not guarantee that vaccines will be effective, that a patient won't have a long wait in the lobby to see the doctor, or that the blood inventory will be adequate. Sometimes, reality overcomes theory.

There is no question that estimating has its power. It can remove unnecessary details, increase efficiency, and is often more understandable and relevant. Still, estimating has its limits. Just this morning, I ran into an old acquaintance in the bank. She said, "I haven't forgotten, I'm going to pay you that hundred dollars for the concert tickets you bought for me last week."

I quickly replied, "Actually, it's $108.78, including tax."

Chapter 32

Caring Matters in the Workplace

March 23, 2024

Wouldn't most agree that it's preferable to be around people who are not only business savvy but are genuinely caring? After all, who wouldn't rather feel good about their interactions with others? Aesop said, "An act of kindness, however small, is never wasted."

Yesterday, I had an uplifting experience. While having lunch in the food court at an upscale shopping mall, I noticed that a mother had left a young child unattended at an adjacent table. I decided to keep my eye on the little girl out of concern for her safety. What happened next was encouraging.

A woman, who manages a specialty food and beverage concession (pastries, gelato, crepes, designer coffees, …), had also noticed the mother leave. She came out from her work area to comfort and reassure the little girl. Her demeanor was very gentle while she stood nearby to ensure the girl's safety. At the same time, she made certain her staff cared for customers.

The mother eventually returned, and the concession manager resumed her work. Her kindness was moving, and I felt the need to tell her as much. She was appreciative. Minutes later the manager came to my table with a gelato cup for me. No charge. She spoke about how she loved her work.

I tried to place a bill in the staff's tip jar, but she would not allow it. Instead, she thanked me for my concern for the girl. Then she made a specialty drink that I ordered and presented it to me as a gift. Her thoughtfulness stood out—to the little girl and to me.

When I thanked her again, she said, "If you extend kindness to people, they will be more likely to extend kindness to others. It will be a better world for all of us to live."

What lessons did I draw from my experience? For one, despite evidence to the contrary, kindness has not disappeared. I'm reminded that in the workplace or otherwise, human needs matter. As a manager, what you sow is what you reap. If you model kindness, loyalty, and respect to customers and subordinates, the work culture will be more likely to reflect this in return.

The experience also reconfirmed to me that there really are angels. Angels have a connotation of being people with high values and virtue. The lady I met was certainly one of them. But angels, to others of us, are also God's messengers. She is one of them.

It is not a revelation to say that people who care are effective in the work environment. But it is worth repeating. They are more effective in their own work, and they set an example for others to follow. Their caring is priceless.

I'm not sure things used to be better. But it seems that way. My parents both grew up on family farms. Though less common today, the family farm community has important parallels for today's business environment.

Everyone on the farm had a job to do and understood the importance of that job to the family. When one could not perform, for whatever reason, the missing link did not go unnoticed. As important, the others stepped in to pick up the slack.

Caring also showed up in community support. When a machine broke down, or hail fell on the field, neighbors showed up to help with field work. When a family member was ill, the same neighbors brought hot meals. They innately knew the importance of supporting each other, inside and outside the family, and they did so willingly.

Has anyone recently left an impression of caring on you as a customer or fellow employee? Have you noticed that someone has gone out of their way to help you or someone else in a business environment? Have you told them how much you appreciate their caring?

I later returned to the concession where the manager was working. She was busy with a customer. One of her staff called me aside and told me, "She is wonderful to work for. My family comes here just to see her. They love her as much as I do."

Humans are selfish by nature, but we can all learn to overcome that tendency and reach out with caring and compassion for others – both at home and at work.

According to Dr. Patrick Flynn, founder of The Wellness Way:

5 HEALTHY BENEFITS OF KINDNESS

REDUCES STRESS AND ANXIETY

MAY REDUCE INFLAMMATION

GIVES YOU MORE ENERGY

REDUCES PAIN

INCREASES LIFESPAN

Chapter 33

Let's Reach a Consensus
February 23, 2024

We have all been to this meeting. The group has spent two hours debating a course of action and a dozen proposals made. But there is no agreement. There is resolute support for Plan A and for Plan B. A smaller group strongly supports Plan C. At this point, someone will inevitably ask "Is there some consensus we can reach here?"

Why should we seek consensus when there is not universal agreement? Warren Buffett has said it is the facts and the correct interpretation of those facts which should lead to a course of action—not whether you are able to get everyone to agree on a course of action. The correct decision should be the goal—not consensus.

The recent debate about vaccinations and masks is a perfect example. Should masks be required? Should they be optional? Should vaccinations be a back-to-work requirement? Should the goal be to save every life or to save the economy for all? Should you be allowed in a restaurant without a mask if you are unvaccinated?

Certain states required masks, others did not. Certain states closed schools, others did not. Certain states closed certain businesses, others did not. Certain states closed churches, others did not. Can you imagine any meeting where consensus was sought?

I remember an experience I had in a healthcare organization. The management group was a diverse and talented team, each member a strong and valuable contributor. Each had a specific sense of the strategy the company should employ, and agreement was difficult to come by. What happened? A consultant was hired to facilitate consensus. The consultant succeeded in securing consensus, but the consensus agreement was a failure.

Where else do we see this? Most prominently in the legislative process. One side proposes its wish list. The other says no, we will only agree to this wish list. They add and subtract until an agreement is reached which will secure the support of most legislators. It is nothing like either side wanted and/or may be unlikely to be good policy. But it secured a consensus. Any examples come to mind?

Abraham Lincoln did not have the unanimous support of his cabinet when he made the Emancipation Proclamation. When he presented the draft of his proposal, at least three of the seven cabinet members opposed or remained silent in the debate. Lincoln did not change his proclamation to secure a consensus. He thought he was right based on the facts.

The next time your group is tempted to seek a consensus, remember Mr. Buffett's theory. One course of action is the right one based on the facts and the correct interpretation of those facts. Seeking unanimity is a mistake.

Chapter 34

What Big Tech Should Actually Do In Healthcare
February 27, 2022

Thank you, Dr. Sachin Jain, for contributing a thought-provoking February 15, 2022, *Forbes* article about "big tech" transforming healthcare. You recommend that Amazon, Google, and Apple buy and transform a large health system.

During my years in the managed health business, I came to see healthcare in America as a "joint venture" among countless, diverse, interested parties—medical groups, physicians, hospitals, urgent care clinics, pharmaceutical companies, and the health plans which bring them together. Each one has a profit incentive independent of the other.

My experience taught me that it is unlikely costs can be contained in a joint venture in healthcare. Each cost control erodes the profit of another entity. Nor is it possible to mingle or "share" the results. Each entity is either profitable or unprofitable on its own. The profitable entities are not interested in sharing their profits with the unprofitable.

I have concluded that the only way in which such a joint venture can work efficiently is for a single entity to control the entire risk pool—to manage the financial results of the entire healthcare enterprise and not be concerned about results for the sub entities. Health plans, even the giants like UnitedHealth Group and Anthem, are primarily organizers. They are unlikely to affect operational costs within, say, a hospital.

But Dr. Jain may have the solution. Apple could do something about those costs. If, as you suggest, Apple owned the entire delivery network of hospitals, physician groups, pharma, the labs, and all that this entails,

Kim Nielsen

they could manage the enterprise cost and deliver effective, coordinated healthcare. And Apple, along with other tech giants, could afford to put it together.

Reflections

Chapter 35

Life Lessons
September 25, 2023

When I grew up, I learned that in America, our freedom of choice included choosing how to respond.

In my first year of college, I learned how to reason, that making assumptions and generalizations about others reflected limited awareness.

In nursing school, I learned how to listen more effectively—as if I would be subject to a deposition after meeting and assessing a patient.

Throughout my career, I've learned that we are not our jobs or our titles. Rather, we are what our jobs allow us to be (along with spiritual bias, God-given talents, family, education, friends, outlook on life, and other factors).

After experiencing losses in my life, I learned who my real friends are and what loyalty and unconditional love means.

In social media, I learned how unimportant "likes" or numbers of connections are. Humble, unassuming people gain my respect. I retreat from arrogance, narcissism and self-absorption. Never make others look small, including ourselves. Include those left on the sidelines.

Throughout life, I've learned to think before speaking, avoid making judgments, and to work to understand others' points of view.

Today, I'm very thankful for persisting in my beliefs, despite public opinion. It doesn't matter if I lose popularity. I'm investing for eternity. People pleasing is a waste of energy.

In my nutrition studies long ago, I learned that eggs do not cause heart disease, avocados are highly nutritious, dark chocolate is not guilt-worthy, but sugar + unhealthy carbs cause chronic inflammation and disease.

My favorite medical finding is that we can alter gene expression through our lifestyle practices. To me, epigenetics is the most exciting field of discovery.

Finally, I need to remember to "be" not only "do" when dividing my time. It seems unlikely that I would wish I had worked more when taking my last breath.

I welcome your thoughts, especially the wisdom YOU have gained.

Chapter 36

Ready to Simplify Life?

July 14, 2021

Is your day, like mine, a never-ending list of to-dos?

Perhaps the name Cyril Northcote Parkinson is familiar to you. Parkinson is remembered for what has become known as Parkinson's Law. His law, first brought to the attention of the public in 1955, proposes that "Work expands to fill the time available for its completion".

Parkinson was a British historian, university professor, and civil servant who observed, in his work, that even simple tasks increased in complexity to fill up the time allotted to them. Conversely, as the length of time allocated to a task became shorter, the task became simpler and easier to solve. Out of those observations came his law.

I am reminded of Professor Parkinson's law when I read an article in the August 6, 2021, edition of the Wall Street Journal entitled Escaping the Efficiency Trap – And Finding Some Peace of Mind, by Oliver Burkeman. The article suggests reorienting your thinking to accept that you will never clear your desk of everything. "The problem with trying to make time for everything that feels important is that you definitely never will." Pretty straight-forward.

According to Burkeman, "… once you stop investing in the idea that you might one day achieve peace of mind that way, it becomes easier to find peace of mind in the present, in the midst of overwhelming demands, because you're no longer making your peace of mind dependent on dealing with all the demands. Once you stop believing that it might somehow be possible to avoid hard choices about time, it gets easier to make better ones."

So, what could you do to increase peace of mind in your workday? It may help to understand Parkinson's Law and accept the recommendations of British journalist Oliver Burkeman. Consider making less time available for work. Get rid of the to-dos that can be eliminated. Then, take time off to enjoy life!

Chapter 37

A Porcelain Bird
September 2, 2021

Every day brings a new set of rules and expectations. Where will I work—at home or in the office? What company will I work for? If I go out, will I have to wear a mask? Will my children be allowed to go to school? Should I get vaccinated? It's easy to become discouraged or even depressed.

If you're an employee, these are the questions you're asking. If you're an employer, these are the questions your employees are asking.

What are you doing differently since the COVID pandemic? How are you making the best of social and occupational change? How have your routines changed? How have your priorities changed?

While contemplating these questions, I read an article by Bill Taylor from The Harvard Business Review. The article addresses managers. The premise is that even optimists experience leadership challenges. But there are means by which they can lift themselves, their colleagues, and their employees. Among them are:

- Insist on crisp execution but make room for "organizational foolishness"
- Invite everyone to become a problem solver, then give them room to fix things
- Don't just champion new ideas; strengthen personal relationships
- To counter bad news, share every piece of good news

This is good advice for every manager, but it's also guidance for everyone who reports to a manager. The article is worth considering.

As I contemplated the article's recommendations, I was reminded of the influence of my grandmother Clara. Clara was a very sociable person whom everyone liked. She was kind and always had something positive to say. But there were times when she preferred to be alone in her own company.

Just outside her front door, she had a small porcelain birdbath on a table. There were four little birds which sat on the rim of the birdbath. Grandma Clara could pivot the birds to face toward or away from the bath.

On days when she would welcome a neighbor for coffee, she faced the birds outward. Neighbors were welcome to visit, and they did. On days when she preferred to be alone, for whatever reason, she faced the birds inward. Her priorities were different that day. Her friends and neighbors knew the formula and respected it. She never had to explain anything. It didn't offend anyone. And no one thought less of her on those days when the birds faced the birdbath.

Through the years, I have tried to develop Grandma Clara's admirable qualities. After reading Taylor's article, I saw the connection to organizational success during difficult times. Grandma Clara was comfortable with "organizational foolishness." Her birds spoke for her. She encouraged others to solve problems; she wasn't always available. She always strengthened her relationships. In fact, people came to her. And she always had good news to share.

She must have inspired the author of the article.

Chapter 38

Veterans Day: Honoring My Father

November 10, 2023

Veterans Day is a day which honors all honorably discharged veterans of military service to the United States. My dad was one.

M. Loquai enlisted in the Marines in 1944. His company of men was among those who assaulted and defeated the Japanese at the island of Iwo Jima in the Pacific Ocean. He was one of only two men from his squad to survive the invasion.

For him, Veterans Day or, as he and his contemporaries knew it, Armistice Day, was an important occasion for him to remind others of the values of this country. He was a patriot. He volunteered as soon as he was eligible and, in later life, shared his love of his country with everyone he met. To my great fortune, I was among them.

As a leader and my father, Dad taught me my values. He made me feel secure, both as my personal protector and a patriotic citizen of the United States. He believed in personal responsibility and accountability in that healthy patriotism includes ongoing devotion to one's country.

Today, forty years after his death, he would be disappointed about the divisiveness and the silliness which has replaced national pride in this country. We argue among ourselves about things which should be obvious. Should we have secure borders? Should we support our strategic allies? Dad was adamant about national security, not whether young boys and girls in our schools should share bathrooms. This represents distraction from our priorities as a nation.

Dad was not one to keep quiet about what he believed. He let you know where he stood. But if someone disagreed with him, he listened then moved on. Had social media been available to him, he would have been appalled by how people hide behind the games on social media (e.g., not "liking" someone's posts), games which reveal pettiness, passive-aggressiveness, and fear of speaking openly.

Every day, I thank God for putting me in the United States, for those who have defended our great country, and for my father for setting a powerfully meaningful example. I'm grateful and proud to be an American and a Loquai. On Veteran's Day, I salute my dad and all veterans for their service.

Chapter 39

Networking is Relationship Building

July 16, 2023

Per Julia Freeland Fisher, Director of Education Research at the Clayton Christensen Institute, CNBC, 2/14/2020: "Research shows that 70 percent of all jobs are not published publicly on jobs sites and as many as eighty percent of jobs are filled through personal and professional connections."

According to Debra Feldman, Executive Talent Agent:

- Networking is not just for when you need to find a new job.
- Every season is the right time for networking relationships.
- It's not just what you know or whom you know, but who knows, likes, and remembers you.

Years ago, I learned the importance of ongoing networking strategies through the extensive experience of a remarkable colleague from Southern California, Jim Kesaris. He taught by example and continues to effectively maintain business and social relationships. I'm thankful for the value he and others provide to exchange ideas and expand opportunities. And I appreciate Jim's recommendation below. It made a difference.

Jim Kesaris
Senior Finance and Operations Executive

Hello Kim,

I've written this recommendation of your work to share with other LinkedIn users.

Kim Nielsen is one of the most respected business managers that I have had the privilege to know and work with. I have known Kim on both a professional and personal basis and have found her to be a person of the highest integrity. She is extremely knowledgeable in her business specialties of healthcare management and administration, strategic planning and execution, and general operations.

Kim provides a unique blend of long-term strategic thinking with common business 'street' sense. Her depth and breadth of experience extends across many related subject areas such as compliance and regulatory affairs, business development and patient services.

Kim has earned the respect of her peers, colleagues and subordinates as a visionary and strategic leader, as well as a hands-on and detail-oriented manager. She leads by example to help meet organizational goals and objectives, while at the same time being very patient-client service oriented.

Furthermore, Kim is very astute and knowledgeable on complex healthcare strategies and related transactions and can articulate the issues with Board members and the executive management team when called upon. She offers very professional and well-researched perspectives when such issues arise.

In addition, Kim possesses the rare combination of exemplary personal attributes, such as: high ethics and moral values, a passion for continued learning, self-discipline and follow-through, and is always well-organized.

Kim is also very generous with her time and technical expertise, volunteering with business networking groups, and supporting various not-for-profit, and charitable organizations, by facilitating and overseeing project work that requires her business expertise and leadership skills.

If you are seeking a creative thinking leader for your senior management team, or dedicated member for your Board, I highly endorse Kim Nielsen for her consummate leadership and integrity, and confident that she will be a dynamic and contributing member, wherever the appropriate opportunity presents itself.

Chapter 40

Overcoming Physician Shortage in the US
September 27, 2021

According to data analysis reported by Health Research Institute at PricewaterhouseCoopers (PwC), the U.S. could face a shortage of as many as 100,000 physicians by 2034. The shortage of physicians and healthcare personnel is not a new problem. The shortage has been described for years. And recommendations by PwC deserve implementation. But there is more that could be done.

First, empower medical schools to accommodate the demand for qualified candidates by opening them up—eliminating quotas. Then, reevaluate the entry requirements. Do the requirements measure what they should be measuring? Are the schools keeping highly qualified candidates out?

Then, find a means to encourage new medical school—especially for-profit models. Emulate the for-profit nursing school model. Professors should teach. The goal should be to graduate competent physicians, not promote primary research. It works for nursing and other professions, why not for physicians?

Second, there should be a complete review and update of medical school curriculum. Make the program more appealing to more candidates. Acknowledge that things have changed. No more 20-hour days, seven days a week. Does a medical student really need to sleep for three hours in a hospital closet because they do not have time to go back to their apartment?

At the same time, emphasize and expand the training of physician assistants. Typically, they are highly skilled at understanding patient presentations to diagnose, treat and manage patient care. Also, emphasize and expand the training of nonphysician practitioners in such areas as nutrition, behavioral health, and physical therapy.

Third, relax rules for physicians and other healthcare providers from other countries. This is the 21st century. The healthcare education and delivery systems of some other countries are just as good or better than those in the U.S. It's easy to check a physician's credentials. If he/she went to a legitimate school, administer a test and a compressed residency requirement. If the applicant passes, welcome him/her to practice medicine. This is also a potential solution to the problem of lack of physicians in rural parts of the U.S.

Fourth, improve the profession. Demand a strengthening of the regulations and continuing education requirements which currently allow unqualified physicians to continue to practice. Encourage honest peer review. Then, demand that legislators change the laws which favor plaintiffs in claims of medical malpractice and diminish the influence of the plaintiff's bar. Who wants to practice medicine with the threat of a lawsuit hanging over every patient encounter?

The solution to the problem of the shortage of physicians is a shared accountability of the medical profession and public policymakers.

~~~

Chapter 41

Environment Impacts Well-Being

April 27, 2023

My unique office is more than an office. It's a sanctuary. It's a place that reflects my stories and those of others who love(d), influence(d), and motivate(d) me. It's also a place where I display the sentimental items and memories which contribute to who I am, and chronicle events that I hold dear. It's emblematic of my life history.

But the contents of my office are not just for me. They're for my loved ones, including my family and life-long friends. Even for unborn generations. In addition to my memories, I hope to convey my compassion for the less fortunate, my devotion to the nursing and wellness professions, and my faith and family values. It's part of my legacy.

Others might put forth their life stories in a different manner. For me, the sanctuary I call my office is a perfect repository representing people and concepts that I treasure.

Chapter 42

Submitting Your Resume
September 15, 2021

Does this sound familiar? You've just spent hours customizing your resume for a position perfectly suited to your experience, skills, and aspirations. Then you spent another hour crafting the perfect cover letter. Finally, you press send.

And then you wait. And wait. You may receive an auto response rejecting your application in less time than it would take to review it. More likely, you get no response. Why would a business waste time applying hands-on talent evaluation skills, when it's both easier and less expensive to allow automated hiring software to reject candidates.

Perhaps this sounds cynical. Then I read today's Wall Street Journal piece written by Kathryn Dill entitled "Companies Need More Workers. Why Do They Reject Millions of Resumes?" Ah ha! It's true. My and your resumes are being ignored in favor of less qualified applicants. The applicant tracking software may make the hiring function easier, but it doesn't find the best candidates. Ms. Dill's article reveals what many have suspected all along, reliance on automated hiring software is counterproductive. She describes a woman who submitted ~ 100 online applications and didn't get a single response. This is a disgrace.

What can we do? First, recognize that online applications will get us next to nowhere. Then, get to work on the most effective means of entry—networking. The best way to gain the attention of the most suitable employer is to get a direct referral. It's what most of us are doing anyway. But it's important to recognize how critical the networking process is and how ineffective the online application process is.

Talk to colleagues, family, friends, neighbors, and acquaintances every day. No exceptions. Tell them what you're looking for. Ask them who they know. Get referrals. If there is a company you want to work for, surely you know someone who works there. Call that person.

Let's not be a victim of the disgrace that Ms. Dill's article reveals.

Chapter 43

Job Satisfaction—Ten Rules to Remember

March 15, 2022

During my more than three decades of employment in the healthcare field, I followed a path that guided me and taught me some important lessons about achieving job satisfaction—mine and others. The valuable reminders below appear in certain discussion forums. Some do not. They all enriched my work experience.

1. Follow your moral compass. Never sacrifice your principles. When in conflict, leave.
2. Make your boss look good. Study how to do it. Then do it.
3. Be a servant leader. Put the growth and performance of those you lead before your own. They will make you look good.
4. Be a generalist, not a specialist. Whatever your job is, seek out knowledge of every aspect of the business you're in. You will be rewarded.
5. Be aware of the job you really want (even if it's not a promotion or not in your company). Get to know and learn from the person who has that job. That person may be leaving soon.
6. When you achieve success (e.g., complete a project ahead of schedule, make a big sale, discover a solution...), do not stop to celebrate. Seek another success. There will be plenty of time to celebrate later.
7. Be bold in your networking. Your network is an essential force in your resource inventory.
8. Great ideas are great. But until they are implemented, they lack greatness. Be the one they come to for great execution.

9. Make yourself vital to the success of your company. Of course, no one is indispensable but that doesn't mean you shouldn't try.
10. The person your employer hires to replace an "irreplaceable" person will potentially be *better* than the person the company replaced. That includes the one who replaces you.

What would you add? What would you remove? Which is most important? Please help improve someone's work experience.

Chapter 44

Quality Standards
February 9, 2024

Throughout my nursing career it has been clear to me that patients are dependent on practitioners who know how to listen and who practice safe and prudent evidence-based medicine.

For example, it was an important part of my critical care training to understand how to accurately auscultate heart sounds (listening for unique and distinct sounds that provide important auditory data about the condition of the heart) and lung sounds (assessing for normal breath sounds vs abnormal breath sounds including crackles, wheezes, pleural friction rub, stridor...). If a practitioner listens to you through your heavy sweatshirt in one lobe of your lung and documents a finding, it's time to question competency. Who wants to wonder if corners were cut in their own care or care of their loved ones?

On a regular basis I am called to triage or offer resources and decision counseling to patients. This morning, a patient contacted me after a disconcerting visit to an overcrowded urgent care in Phoenix. He was seen for evaluation of an ongoing upper respiratory infection with frequent cough and fever. He described being asked if he wanted a Covid test without receiving a physical exam of his chest, throat, or sinuses. There was no physical assessment.

Is this the standard of care we should expect? Do you suppose the urgent care will bill him? Easy answer. Why are patients put in a position to diagnose and treat themselves and pay a significant fee for a service they haven't received in association with reliable medical care?

Why did I go into nursing in the first place? Easy. I want to protect patients. I want them to be understood, treated safely with dignity, and to have individualized care that reflects thorough clinical evaluation and advice.

I always remember Reed V. Tuckson, M.D., F.A.C.P., Executive Vice President and Chief of Medical Affairs for UnitedHealth Group and Senior Vice President for Professional Standards of the AMA, presenting at a medical director conference. He described his personal goal to have every patient treated and cared for with the standards he wanted for his own mother, consistent with the AMA's mission to ameliorate suffering in every patient.

Is Tuckson's admonition too much to ask for in every healthcare setting?

Chapter 45

Happy Earth Day 2021
April 22, 2021

The next time you hear Alexandria Ocasio-Cortez or Bernie Sanders railing about climate change and the need to eliminate fossil fuels, please listen to the thoughts of a truly socially conscious investor who is also an energy expert.

Jeff Ubben is the co-founder of Inclusive Capital Partners, a fund that invests in companies which are "…not green yet…" but can be. He believes that "… working with management teams and boards with the courage to lead on solutions to climate change and social inequity can generate massive shareholder value."

He was recently elected to the Board of Directors of Exxon Mobil, an unlikely place, it would seem, for an ESG activist. He believes that, by itself, industry can get to net zero carbon emissions, exclusive of transport and industrial. With subsidies less than those of EVs (electric vehicles), carbon can be profitably captured from the 50 percent of energy demand allocated to transport and industrial use. Thus, a combination of private sector ingenuity and government subsidy consistent with that of EVs, can get us to net zero.

If, like me, you feel there must be something better than the mind-numbing prattling about the Green New Deal, listen to Jeff Ubben's interviews for a common sense, if somewhat technical, discussion of an alternative solution to the problem of carbon emissions. Greta Thunberg need not go further.

Chapter 46

Housing Market Quandaries

May 27, 2021

Kelly Evans, CNBC anchor, said that the housing market is "insane." Is it? Or is it another leg in a cycle?

It's not breaking news that home prices have increased substantially in 2021. I drive around my neighborhood, and where I see a For Sale sign, I also see a line of potential buyers. This occurred in California in 1988 as well. Then, people entered lotteries just to have the privilege of paying skyrocketing prices for homes. How long did the frenzy last? In one Dana Point neighborhood, 44 homes were placed under contract through a lottery in 1988. By the time construction was completed in late 1989, one home had closed escrow with the original buyer. The other 43 "buyers" had all walked away from their contracts, and the development looked like a ghost town. The market had collapsed.

In 2006-2007, when anyone with a pulse could get a loan due to liberal mortgage loan underwriting, people, some without jobs, bid up the prices of homes with the expectation they would live off the rents and increasing values. My neighbor's home was owned by such an "investor." That investor owned three homes in the neighborhood. How long did that frenzy last? By late 2009, all three of his homes were in foreclosure and he was in bankruptcy. The housing collapse which began in 2008 has been well-chronicled.

From the highs of 1988 and 2006, and the subsequent collapses, it took years for home prices to recover. Why is today different from 1988 or 2006? Ms. Evans presents her insight in this article entitled "The Housing Market Is Insane."

My opinion as to why 2021 is different. Buyers are reported to want to own the homes they are bidding on currently. Many are not speculating or "investing" (prices may be too high for speculators). Buyers appear to be seeking a home for their families.

Why are they willing to pay the higher prices? They recognize that they are in competition with like-minded buyers, not speculators, and are afraid that prices may be even higher next year. Also, remote and hybrid work environments are encouraging mobility—people are moving to where they want to live, not where the job is. Demand is shifting away from traditional employment centers to lower-cost areas or "places I've always wanted to live."

Ms. Evans is correct in concluding that, this time, we are experiencing a structural shift and not simply a cyclical phenomenon. Although homes are being sold for premium prices, the number being sold is far from excessive. Insane or not, for the above reasons, and if mortgage loan underwriting continues to be strict, the higher prices in the current buying frenzy are likely to continue.

*Kelly Evans is anchor of CNBC's "The Exchange" (M-F, 1PM-2PM ET), the newsroom-based program for today's investor. She is also co-anchor of CNBC's "Power Lunch," which broadcasts from the network's headquarters in Englewood Cliffs, NJ.

Chapter 47

Boundaries

December 4, 2021

Lance Morrow is a frequent and welcome contributor to the *Wall Street Journal.* In his opinion piece entitled "An Age of Violated Boundaries" from a November 2021 edition of the *WSJ*, he points out that the southern border of the United States, personal privacy, the notion that one is either male or female, and city police protecting the citizenry are examples of boundaries that no longer exist.

As these conventions disintegrate, does what replaces them improve our society? Are we better off not enforcing our borders and allowing thousands to illegally cross the border into Texas? Do we feel safer now that police are ordered to allow anarchy in major cities because the crime is "victimless" or committed by the "underprivileged"?

Do people feel more empowered now that they can select whichever gender suits them? Should non-citizens be allowed to vote? Are we better prepared to unite as a country and prevent terrorism?

Mr. Morrow presents an enlightened alternative to the contemporary media (and woke society) point of view. I appreciate his contribution and clarity.

Chapter 48

Any Interest in I Bonds?

February 2, 2022

Little publicized but potentially valuable, United States Treasury Department I Bonds may have a place in your investment portfolio.

These bonds have an unusual feature. They carry two separate interest rates. The first is a fixed rate. It's guaranteed for the life of the bond. The second is an inflation rate which is adjusted every six months. The sum of the two is what you are paid.

What are the rates today? On bonds issued today (2/2/22), the fixed rate is zero, about what checking accounts are earning. But the inflation rate is over 7 percent. Worth thinking about. They are issued for 30 years but can be redeemed at any time after the first year.

About the only thing that is disappointing about I Bonds is the limit on purchase; each purchaser is limited to $10,000 per year. Nevertheless, even with guaranteed rate of zero, a couple with the ability to set aside $10,000 each, every year for ten years, would have accumulated over $224,000— assuming just a 2.5 percent inflation rate. Since the redemption value is never less than the face amount, there is no interest rate risk to your principal. Remember, the inflation rate changes every six months.

Check out "TreasuryDirect" for the fine print. If I Bonds are of interest to you, they are simple to purchase through an easily opened Treasury Direct account.

Chapter 49

Cryptoviral Extortion
February 18, 2024

Scammers and hackers are going after more than individuals now—targeting big companies and even school systems, hospitals, and medical facilities. Cryptoviral extortion is the shady process that encrypts the victim's files, making them inaccessible and demands a ransom payment to decrypt them. Specifically, these criminals demand huge extortion payments or threaten to destroy entire companies. Our power sources and water supplies are already threatened. Colonial Pipeline just paid $5 million to come back online. (The fact that the FBI recovered the payment does not diminish the risk.)

The world has become reliant on computer technology to run most aspects of our lives. This has become the new frontier of law-breaking. Criminals know this and sense opportunity. Africa has long been the base for online criminals targeting individuals. Experienced extortionists are also based in Russia or China. The next ransom demand could result in the deaths of millions of people.

According to Melissa D. Berry, Lead Compliance Attorney Editor, Thomson Reuters, 7/5/22: "Because healthcare organizations are so heavily dependent on access to data — such as patient records—to maintain their operations, they are a frequent target for ransomware attacks. Even a short delay in access to records can result in negative outcomes for patients."

Because addressing the problem of cybercrime is in the national interest, a partnership between the federal government and private industry will be essential. In America, public trust in the government remains low.

Kim Nielsen

But private industry, to be successful, will require the resources only the federal government can assemble. Together, however, the partnership could be formidable.

It is ironic. The modern technology that frees us from problems leads to newer problems which, in turn, threaten to make us less and less free as individuals. State-sponsored criminals are no different from the enemies in war. They need to be defeated.

Chapter 50

No Regrets: Make Your Dreams Come True

May 8, 2023

The healthiest people I know take time to follow their dreams. The attached photos document my dream vacation. All during just a couple of days off.

Many people live their lives for 'someday.' They put their dreams on hold, waiting for the right time, not realizing that someday may never come. - Anthon St. Maarten

Work hard, enjoy life, have no regrets.

Chapter 51

Gingerbread House

February 9, 2024

When my children grew up, we lived next door to Dave, the Superintendent of the Minneapolis School District. Every year, he blessed us with a new creative gingerbread house on Christmas Eve. We were always excited to hear the doorbell ring to see his creation since he spent the better part of a day building and decorating an elaborate piece of art. This became a memory associated with kindness, caring, and generosity.

Being surprised is a special gift, and being remembered is invaluable.

Image by Angela from Pixabay

Academia

Chapter 52

Intro to Capstone Project
November 28, 2011

In November 2011, I completed a research paper advocating a single-payer healthcare system in the United States. Since then, Obamacare principles (Affordable Care Act) resulted in more people being insured by health benefits – primarily Medicaid. Yet, the demand for a single-payer system persists with a large segment of the population and the political spectrum. Three factors contribute to understanding the problem and potential solutions.

Healthcare Availability

Though healthcare is not automatic, Medicaid, Medicare, and private insurance, in combination, have made healthcare available to all but 7.7 percent of the US population (according to an August 2023 statement by the CDC). In addition, hospitals must treat emergencies for patients with or without insurance.

But this care is not problem-free. Just look at the emergency department waiting rooms. They resemble the DMV. And in sections of the country, few physicians treat Medicare patients, making access to care problematic.

By contrast, certain European countries provide healthcare for all people though most require copays. Norway, Finland, Sweden, Denmark, and Iceland pay 100 percent of the cost with no added out-of-pocket expense to the patient.

Healthcare Delivery

In the United States, doctors are independent practitioners or are employed by a healthcare business. They are not employed by the government. As such, they can usually choose to treat whichever patients they wish, subject to anti-discrimination laws. In countries such as Finland, all healthcare practitioners are employed by the government. The next logical step after single pay is to make health practitioners government employees. Physicians and hospitals would resist such systems in a free-market society such as the United States.

Healthcare Financing

Today, healthcare in the U.S. is financed by a combination of private insurance (through employers or self-pay), government plans (Medicaid, and Medicare, and state plans), direct-pay fee-for-service, and other third-party sources.

In many countries, the government finances all healthcare using general tax revenues. Proposals in this country would have the federal government pay for all care. The source of funds would be the general revenues of the federal government, an enormous tax increase.

Any solution involving a single payer must address all three factors. Otherwise, it is unworkable.

Chapter 53

Capstone Paper

UNIVERSAL HEALTHCARE

Professional Research Project: Universal Healthcare Access

Kim Nielsen

Grand Canyon University

November 28, 2011

Kim Nielsen

Abstract

The United States spends a greater portion of its gross domestic product on healthcare than any other country yet many individuals have limited access to care and others cannot afford it. Ample evidence exists to support a universal access, single-payer, privately-delivered healthcare system as being more effective than the status quo, a single-payer, government-delivered system or other systems used elsewhere in the world. The proposal presented in this research paper requires legislation by the U. S. Congress and may require establishment of a new, cabinet-level department of government. Thus, implementation of universal access would be an enormous and costly national undertaking. Under the proposal put forth in this paper, universal access means that everyone in the United States would have an equal availability of healthcare - assuring all Americans benefits similar to those received by Medicare beneficiaries today. When fully in place, this program would provide healthcare access to 50,000,000 individuals who are currently uninsured. Evaluation of the success of the program will require data to be analyzed assessing three variables - patient health, cost of care and nurse staffing. To evaluate changes in patient health, the CMS Office of Clinical Standards and Quality would develop brief self-assessments for newly insured patients and similar patient assessments for the nurse. To evaluate cost of care, CMS would develop tools to measure how costs are performing relative to expectations and to other populations. To evaluate increases in nurse staffing, regular employment reporting would be required. Disseminating the results of these evaluations to the nursing community serves to facilitate communication and understanding of the significance of universal access. Understanding should include the value being added to patient health and the nursing profession. Nurses must remain convinced that, under universal access, improved patient care through more nurses is a goal rather than more patient care with fewer nurses. The nursing profession is ideally suited to inform both patients and healthcare professionals. Universal access to healthcare financed by the federal government and delivered locally by private physicians and hospitals is a socially desirable goal of the United States. By adopting such a program, the United States will join the other industrialized nations of the world in providing all citizens with affordable healthcare. No one, however, has a greater stake in this outcome than today's uninsured population for whom a solution would be a lifeline to healthcare.

Key words: universal access, single-payer, uninsured.

Professional Research Project: Universal Healthcare Access

There is only one major country in the industrialized world where citizens lack universal access to healthcare - the United States (Landers & Leeman, 2011). Healthcare is financed by a mix of private insurance, principally arranged by employers, and by government plans. Individuals who are not eligible for government plans or who are uninsured at work are left to arrange for and pay for care. Although many proposed solutions have been put forth, none has been adopted to date. Universal access to healthcare would be an enormous undertaking - legislatively, administratively, financially and, perhaps most important, with patients, physicians and nurses.

Notwithstanding the obstacles, a proposal will be presented in this paper which purports to satisfy the many competing interests and needs. The solution will have a significant effect on newly insured patients and health professionals. Following implementation, this proposal will provide access to care for millions of people currently lacking healthcare.

Identifying the Problem

Throughout America, individuals in need of healthcare are left without access to or the means to pay for adequate care (Landers & Leeman, 2011). Care is unevenly distributed throughout the population and many people have no insurance to pay for health services (Tanner, 2008). The mechanisms for funding healthcare in the United States leave a large segment of the population isolated from care which is readily accessible by individuals with some form of public or private insurance (Landers & Leeman, 2011).

Healthcare is a topic of ongoing debate (Hoffman, 2011). The United States spends a greater portion of its gross domestic product on healthcare than any other country (Tanner, 2008). Yet, many individuals have limited access to care and others cannot afford it. According to the U. S. Census Bureau, as shown in APPENDIX A, the population of uninsured individuals in America - those without some plan to pay for their healthcare - is approximately 50 million (DeNavas-Walt, Proctor, & Smith, 2011). To the extent this population lacks the resources to pay for care, the uninsured individuals may be precluded from receiving care. The issue is primarily one of access and affordability - not quality. For those who have coverage, healthcare in America is quite accessible and of high quality. For those who do not, healthcare is anything but adequate. Some alternative to the status quo is necessary.

A comprehensive plan to finance the cost of healthcare for everyone would have an enormous impact on the public and the nursing profession. A plan making healthcare available to all would immediately bring nurses together with patients who have never before had complete access to care. Hospitals and medical offices would experience a new population of patients with previously untreated conditions. This would be of great benefit to previously uninsured individuals. Such a plan would challenge existing nursing capacity and other healthcare professionals as well as open opportunities for new nurses.

There are many competing issues to be understood and resolved when addressing the matter of the uninsured. Even among proponents of some sort of universal system, there is no agreement on which healthcare services should be covered (Hoffman, 2011). Several approaches have been proposed - each containing strengths and limitations (Glied, 2009). None has emerged as the popular choice.

One approach, however, merits consideration. Called the single-payer system, this approach would radically alter the means by which healthcare is financed. Though not new, this is proposed as an alternative to the status quo and other choices. Under such a system, the government would pay for all covered healthcare, for all citizens, out of payroll and income taxes. Private and local community-operated hospitals as well as independent physicians and other professionals would continue to be responsible for the delivery of all healthcare (Guzmano, Weisz, & Rodwin, 2009).

No ideal solution satisfies all stakeholders. Nevertheless, ample evidence exists to support a recommendation of a universal access, single-payer, privately-delivered healthcare system. The following proposal is posited in PICOT question format: For American citizens (P), is a universal access, single-payer, privately-delivered healthcare system (I), implemented over two years (T), more effective than a) the status quo, b) a single-payer, government-delivered system or c) systems used elsewhere in the world (C) in assuring high-quality, affordable healthcare (O)?

Implementation

Universal access to care for all Americans financed by the federal government and delivered by private physicians and hospitals would provide a solution to what is an alarming social deficiency in the United States. APPENDIX A shows that both the number and percent of the population without health insurance have been increasing (DeNavas-Walt et al., 2011). The gross domestic product of the United States was $14.5 trillion in 2010, the highest in the world (The World Bank, 2011a). The same data source showed that the United States spends 16.2 percent of gross domestic product on healthcare (The World Bank, 2011b). Nevertheless, despite the United States spending a greater portion of gross domestic product on healthcare than any other developed country in the world, 50 million individuals are uninsured.

The United States is the only major country without universal access to healthcare (Landers & Leeman, 2011). As a result, 16 percent of Americans do not have immediate access to care (DeNavas-Walt et al., 2011). With the average cost of health insurance exceeding $12,000 annually per family, healthcare quality is unevenly distributed among the population (Tanner, 2008).

According to DeNavas-Walt et al. (2011), most individuals in America, 55.3 percent, are covered by health insurance arranged by employers. Medicare covers most adults over age 65 (Medicare.gov, 2011). Medicaid covers individuals with household incomes below 138 percent of the Federal

Poverty Level (Landers & Leeman, 2011). The Medicare and Medicaid programs are financed by payroll and income taxes with healthcare being delivered by independent hospitals and physicians. Notwithstanding, 16 percent of Americans are without coverage.

The means by which healthcare is accessed, financed and delivered in other countries varies. According to Tanner (2008), in information covering ten major industrial countries as shown in APPENDIX B, only the United States lacks universal access. In some countries, individuals are required to purchase insurance whereas in others, the government finances insurance for everyone. Switzerland, The Netherlands and Japan feature a multi-payer system – similar to the United States. All others have a single-payer system of financing. Outside the United States, reimbursement rates are established by the government and, in most cases, there are waiting lists. Only in the U.K. is healthcare delivered primarily by government employees. Significantly, the U.K. has one of the longest reported waiting lists.

Various proposals have been made to address this condition. Proposals include universal access, single-payer financing, multi-payer financing, government-delivered healthcare, privately-delivered healthcare and maintaining the status quo. Each has its proponents and detractors. None has gained overwhelming favor.

Under the proposal put forth in this paper, universal access means that everyone in America would have equal access to healthcare benefits. Equal access would assure all Americans benefits similar to those experienced by Medicare beneficiaries today. Single-payer means that the federal government, through payroll and income taxes, finances the entire cost of this program. Individuals would pay a fair share through co-pays, co-insurance and the tax system. Neither employers, insurance companies nor health plans would play a part in financing health insurance, only the government.

Privately-delivered healthcare means that the system will be unchanged from that in place today. Private hospitals and independent physicians will continue to deliver care. The government will not employ physicians nor operate hospitals. Government's role will be to finance care, not provide it.

The importance of equal access to care cannot be overstated. Tanner (2008) found equal access to be more important than quality in Germany and France. The physicians sampled by McCormick et al. (2009) also emphasized the need for guaranteed access. Under this proposal, each individual would have guaranteed health insurance and would have equal access to care.

Another recommendation for universal access is opportunity to reduce administrative costs. Bentley, Effros, Palar, & Keeler (2008) and Glied (2009) both conclude that a principal goal of a single-payer system is to make health insurance less costly and more efficient. Cost efficiency is another reason to support the single-payer concept.

In any universal access system, a critical feature is the healthcare delivery. Countries such as the U.K. and Norway, where most care is delivered by government-employed physicians and government-owned facilities, regularly experience long waiting times (Tanner, 2008). Waiting lists are not mentioned in countries with fully-private delivery such as the United States, Switzerland or France. Clearly, government delivery systems contribute to waiting lists. This proposal supports private delivery.

A survey of physician groups in the United States supports private delivery of healthcare - even in a single-payer environment. Bitton, Martin & Landon (2010) described a privately-operated organization of multi-specialty medical facilities caring for five million people and paid through capitation. One conclusion was that public policy interest in this type of financing and delivery is growing. No support, however, could be found for a "socialized medicine" approach such as that of the U.K. or Norway. Considerable evidence and data exist to support the proposal in this paper. Bentley et al. (2008) and Glied (2009) both cited data demonstrating a reduction in administrative costs. Cooper (2009) concludes that more spending yields higher quality of care. Since the United States spends a greater percent of gross domestic product on healthcare than any other developed nation in the world, one might conclude that quality in the United States system is high relative to other countries (World Bank, 2011b). Tanner (2008) concurs saying "...the United States provides the world's highest quality healthcare..." (p. 33).

Another reason for supporting the proposal is the provision of equitable access to care. Research by Gusmano, Weisz, & Rodwin (2009) concluded that universal coverage has a great deal to do with equal access. Hsuei-Chen et al. (2010) also found in research that a single-payer system assured equitable access to the treatment studied.

The potential for catastrophic out-of-pocket costs to patients was researched by Ke et al. (2007). The researchers concluded that in a universal access, single-payer system risk of financial catastrophe to patients is lowered. This supports the goal of making affordable healthcare available to all.

Finally, research by McCormick et al. (2009) sampled the opinion of 3,400 physicians in direct patient care practice. Eighty-nine percent believed that individuals should receive necessary care regardless of ability to pay - a universal access system. Only nine percent would preserve the status quo. Implementation of universal access would be an enormous national undertaking. Responsibility would fall most heavily on two broadly defined groups - the government and the private healthcare delivery system. At the government level, the first step would be the passage of legislation. Conducting research, holding hearings, convening town-hall meetings, gaining popular support and passing legislation could take two years or more.

In a hospital, administration and management must be shown evidence of the need for a practice change before implementation. In contrast, the proposal presented in this paper requires approval of the U. S. Congress. The organization to which this proposal will apply is not a hospital but the entire nation. The use of the rational choice theory will help bring the major constituents together in a consensus. The rational choice theory "states that individuals base their decisions on the expectation of maximizing their profits and minimizing their costs..." (Akers, 1994, as cited in Mason & Monk-Turner, 2010, p. 560).

Lawmakers, the public, patients, physicians, nurses and hospital administrators will likely reach the proposed conclusion by recognizing that the sociological benefits of the proposal outweigh the costs. Using rational choice theory as the basis for decision-making, thought leaders will crystallize public thinking into a popular solution. By approaching the problem from the perspective of rational choice theory, the solution should become clear and a groundswell of popular support should result in legislation.

Such legislation may require establishment of a new, cabinet-level department of government. Alternatively, a substantial expansion of the existing department of Health and Human Services (the administrators of Medicare and Medicaid) would be necessary. Once a law is passed, crafting and writing numerous regulations would follow. Setting up a nationwide administrative capacity and public orientations as to program specifics would be next.

At the delivery level, private hospitals and medical groups must also gear up for new patients, new systems and new bureaucracy. Although affecting some medical groups and hospitals more than others, an increase of 50 million patients will require a commitment to new hiring, new training and investment in technology. The new environment will require hiring many new nurses and physicians. Nurses will be faced with an entirely new group of patients, many of whom have delayed adequate healthcare. Not only will more nurses be needed but the number of nursing programs must be increased. Both resources will be critical to caring for the new population.

In addition to these logistics, several obstacles will have to be addressed which cannot be fully anticipated prior to implementation. First, both O'Neill & O'Neill (2007) and Tanner (2008) describe waiting lists, rationing and limits on physician choice in countries with universal access, single-payer systems - especially countries more heavily weighted toward government control. It will be essential to closely monitor care delivery and be alert for developing waiting lists. Furthermore, Hsuei-Chen et al. (2010), Korda et al. (2009) and O'Neill & O'Neill (2007) raise questions as to whether access to and quality of care are adequately assured in a single-payer, universal system. Data must be maintained and evaluated addressing those questions.

Increased bureaucracy is a threat to efficiency. Buerhaus (2010) reported that economist Paul Feldstein warned of decreases in the efficiency of the health system under single-payer. Tanner (2008) urged that this country learn "…from the experiences of other countries, which demonstrate the failure of centralized command and control…" (p. 1). Finally, although cost reduction is anticipated in a single-payer system, Newhouse & Sinaiko (2007) question whether lower costs would actually occur in a government-operated financing system.

The largest single new physical resource will be the federal administrative staff required to support this program. Medicare is a likely model. Under Medicare, ten regional offices of the Centers for Medicare and Medicaid Services (CMS) pay all claims to providers and provide benefit information for 90 million enrollees (Medicare.gov, 2011). With this additional staffing will come the need for administrative forms, documents and benefit brochures.

At present, existing technology and systems in the CMS should be sufficient to manage the new program. Eligibility is already being verified. Claims are already being paid. Healthcare providers are being contracted and having credentials checked. The only requirement is expansion to accommodate 50 million additional individuals. Assessing effectiveness of the new universal system will require time for gathering and evaluating data. Once credible data is available, studies such as cost-per-patient, before-and-after administrative costs, mortality studies, morbidity studies and disease-specific outcomes research should be conducted.

Finally, there is the financial cost of healthcare for everyone. With 50 million uninsured individuals at an average cost of healthcare per person of $4,479, the initial annual cost to the federal treasury will be approximately $225 billion (Tanner, 2008). This represents over 8 percent of the expected 2012 Treasury Department revenues of $2.63 trillion (Office of Management and Budget, 2010).

Evaluation

The program being measured is universal access, single-payer financed, privately delivered healthcare. When the program is implemented, physicians, nurses, newly insured patients, hospital administrators and the public will share a vision for success and have a stake in the results. Because the subject of this paper is patients and nurses, only the effect on those stakeholders will be addressed.

Meaningful data is fundamental to healthcare decisions (Fineout-Overholt & Johnson, 2007). In the case of universal access, a determination will be made as to what, if any, results occurred because of implementation (Melnyk & Fineout-Overholt, 2011). This program will require data to be collected locally and analyzed on a national basis. The program is national with locally delivered care. The CMS will perform a major role in the gathering, analysis and dissemination of program results. CMS, among other things, is the federal agency which administers Medicare and Medicaid and provides information for health professionals and consumers (U. S. Department of Health and Human Services, 2011).

An analysis of the data will be conducted to assess three variables. Included are patient health, cost of care and nurse staffing. Each of these is an important component of the proposal and evaluation will be necessary.

One assumption of the proposal is that with universal access to care, health of the beneficiaries will improve. Patient health will be assessed longitudinally - both by the patient and a nurse. The primary focus of the assessment will be change of health status. Another proposal assumption is that healthcare would become more cost effective. Cost of care data will be assembled by the CMS which is also responsible for payment for healthcare and is perfectly suited to determine trends in costs. A third assumption is that nurse employment will increase as a result of the newly insured patient population. Regulation-based nurse staffing reporting would be required of all hospitals and medical groups to verify that assumption.

A nationwide evaluation of this data will be essential. Under the program envisioned, the CMS would most likely be the focal point. That organization would aggregate and analyze the data and reach appropriate conclusions. Eventually, however, reports from the evaluation will be especially important to nurses and, therefore, patients at point-of-service (Melnyk & Fineout-Overholt, 2011). Thus, program analyses will be distributed regularly by the CMS to every participating medical group and hospital.

The method by which patient health will be measured is by self-assessment at time of first encounter and self-assessment at a subsequent future date two years later. Patient-reported assessments "...provide information unavailable from other sources…that is critical for predicting health outcomes…" (Baiardini et al., 2009, p.290). Similar assessments will be made at the same times by a nurse. Changes in health status will reveal the effectiveness of universal access. Cost of care will be determined and assessed by the CMS using actual versus expected unit cost information. Overall cost effectiveness can be determined by comparing actual costs with patient/nurse health improvement assessments. By doing so, researchers will be able to calculate the actual cost of improving patient health. Finally, changes in nurse staffing will be determined through mandatory reports to the CMS by each hospital and medical group.

Means to educate all major stakeholders are necessary although only nurses and patients will be addressed in this paper. To educate the nurses, teams of representatives from the CMS would conduct seminars throughout the country. These seminars would describe the role of nurses in patient data collection. Nursing staffs would send delegates to these seminars. The responsibility of the delegates would be to learn, understand and bring back the information. The delegates would then convey the learning to the remaining nursing staff. Patients will be informed by nurses.

These CMS seminars would also be an excellent opportunity to educate nurses about the data that will be reported and maintained on nurse employment. Increased nursing employment is a goal of the proposal. Ongoing communication of trends in nursing employment will be important to maintain the support of nurses for the program.

Specific tools, primarily developed by the government, will be needed to evaluate the outcomes of this program. To evaluate changes in patient health, the CMS Office of Clinical Standards and Quality would develop two tools - a brief self-assessment for newly insured patients and a similar patient assessment for the nurse, each taking approximately 30 minutes to complete. The tools would be completed by patient and nurse at the time of the patient's first encounter with the practice and, again, two years later. Preparation and submission of these assessments would be a condition of payment for the provider.

To evaluate cost of care, CMS would develop a tool to establish how costs are performing relative to expectations and other populations. Comparing the actual cost data with that of Medicare, Medicaid, commercially insured groups and, perhaps most important, other countries would provide benchmarks. In a study by Beyan & Baykal (2010), the researchers described an original framework for the comparison of various care and health system performance measures. A similar framework might form the basis of the CMS analysis.

To evaluate nurse staffing, reports would be made a part of the routine transfer of information and funds between the facilities and the CMS. As shown in APPENDIX C, hospitals and medical groups would provide data on nurse employment reflecting staff turnover, age of nurses, length of employment and credentials. With the data from this tool, the effect on employment in the community of nurses, as a result of universal access, can be determined.

Dissemination

Once universal access is adopted, communication of content to stakeholders will follow. Disseminating evidence serves to facilitate communication and adoption of findings into nursing practice (Oermann, Galvin, & Floyd, 2006, as cited in Melnyk & Fineout-Overholt, 2011). Nurses must have confidence describing the new program to patients and understand the impact on nursing employment.

Nurse delegates will have received an orientation from CMS. A problem with evidence-based results is that, too often, they are not communicated (Melnyk & Fineout-Overholt, 2011). These delegates will disseminate findings to their constituencies for implementation into practice. Dissemination may take place through personal presentations, panel discussions, printed material and/or community forums.

Dissemination of most patient-related evidence will take place during examination or treatment. Newly insured patients will receive one-on-one explanations of the benefits of the new program. Patients will also be oriented to the before-and-after health assessments.

This dissemination of evidence must be well-prepared. Whether to nurses or to patients, presentations must be based on sound evidence and include written summaries for hand-out. Presentations must be conducted on a timely basis to help nurses make appropriate decisions (Grand Canyon University, n.d.). Advance notices of community meetings will improve attendance.

Barriers to successful dissemination include lack of time, language barriers and apathy. Lack of reading time was cited by Walsh (2010) as the greatest barrier to evidence-based practice use. Nursing workloads may make scheduling presentations difficult. Moreover, newly insured patients may speak a different language than the nurse. Apathy is a risk to implementing any new program. Because of the importance of disseminated information to patient care, these barriers must be overcome. The significance of universal access must be understood by the nursing community. This includes an understanding of the value being added to patient health and the nursing profession. Patient health is promoted significantly by gaining access to care. Many new patients will not have previously had regular healthcare. The nursing community, through professional organizations, must add to the outreach to bring as many new patients as possible into a physician's office. Once in a clinical setting, newly insured patients must be shown the value of healthcare. Nurses should be recognized by these patients as highly-skilled, caring professionals.

The nursing profession is promoted through more employment opportunities. New patients imply new jobs. Results from nurse staffing reports should be clearly communicated to the nurse community - nationally, statewide, locally and in the work setting. Improving employment opportunities for nurses must be appreciated to assure continued support for universal access. Nurses must be convinced that, under universal access, improved patient care through more nurses is a goal rather than more patient care with fewer nurses.

Conclusion

Many people in America have no access to healthcare due to high cost and inability to pay. The status quo, a multi-payer, non-universal healthcare system, is the deficiency. To properly address that deficiency, evidence supports that the United States must implement a healthcare system in which all individuals have coverage - a universal access system - and simplify the payment mechanism into a single-payer system. By doing so, the United States will join the other industrialized nations of the world in providing citizens with affordable healthcare for all.

The proposal presented in this paper requires approval of the U. S. Congress as well as the people and would be a considerable administrative and financial undertaking. By recognizing that the sociological benefits of the proposal outweigh the costs, lawmakers, the public, patients, physicians, nurses and hospital administrators will reach the proposed conclusion. Only then will all Americans enjoy universal access to healthcare.

When the universal access program is initiated, processes must be in place to evaluate results. Whether health status of previously uninsured patients is improving, whether the new program is performing as anticipated financially and whether employment opportunities for nurses are improving are just a few of the important questions to answer.

Disseminating evidence to newly insured patients, nurses and the nursing community will also be necessary. Nurses and patients need to be informed. The nursing profession is ideally suited to inform both patients and professionals.

Universal access to healthcare is an important social issue in America and has yet to be resolved. Nurses, physicians and other healthcare providers all have a large stake in the solution. None, however, have a greater stake than today's uninsured population for whom a solution would be a lifeline to healthcare.

Annotated Bibliography

Article1:

Barr, D. A. (2007). A research protocol to evaluate the effectiveness of public-private partnerships as a means to improve health and welfare systems worldwide. *American Journal of Public Health, 97*(1), 19-25. doi:10.2105/AJPH.2005.075614

This article reviewed the history of public-private partnerships, which focus on addressing specific serious diseases. The purpose was to determine if these types of partnerships are effective and if expanding the use of these partnerships should include a wider range of diseases. The peer-reviewed descriptive research addressed the growth of public-private partnerships and the disease subjects of the partnerships.

The study concludes that there is no clear evidence that such partnerships should be expanded until additional research is conducted. The conclusions reached in the article are neither favorable nor unfavorable to the single-payer system. Such partnerships do impact nursing and patient care through an expansion of health services to affected patients. More patients receive care from more nurses.

Article 2:

Bentley, T., Effros, R., Palar, K., & Keeler, E. (2008). Waste in the United States health care system: A conceptual framework. *Milbank Quarterly, 86*(4), 629-659.

Waste is seen as a significant contributor to the cost of healthcare in America. This systematic review was conducted in attempt to determine causes and recommend reforms to achieve appropriate expense reduction. One such recommendation for policymakers is the adoption of cost-saving techniques, such as employed in a Canadian-style single payer system. The study analyzed sources of expenditure and compared them within various countries, concluding that the American system has the highest level of administrative costs.

The authors favor a single-payer system. The main recommendation is implementation of reforms, which would make health insurance and healthcare more efficient and less costly. The implication for nursing and patients is that with lower costs, more people will be able to afford insurance and be cared for. This means more demand for and employment of nurses.

Article 3:

Bitton, A., Martin, C., & Landon, B. E. (2010). A nationwide survey of patient centered medical home demonstration projects. *JGIM: Journal of General Internal Medicine*, *25*(6), 584-592. doi:10.1007/ s11606-010-1262-8

The subject of this article is the emerging concept of patient centered medical homes (PCMHs) where a physician group provides all primary and specialty care in exchange for a capitation (or some hybrid). This is a form of single-payer system — the subject of this writer's proposal —

and currently involves over five million patients. This descriptive research reported on data from a group of representative PCMHs, concluding that public policy interest in this financing and delivery system is growing.

The conclusions reached in the article support a single-payer system. The implication for nurses and patients is the same for any proposal including single-payer financing – more patients with healthcare and more nurses employed. Alternatively, there is possible system overload resulting in overworked nurses and lower quality of patient care.

Article 4:

Buerhaus, P. I. (2010). Is United States health care evolving toward a single-payer system? An interview with health care economist Paul Feldstein, PhD. *Nursing Economic$*, *28*(3), 198-201.

This article reports on an interview with a renowned healthcare economist. The economist describes the pros and cons of a single-payer system and provides expert opinion. One conclusion is that the best approach to healthcare financing is not necessarily a single-payer system which decreases incentives for efficiency.

A system which eliminates the current employer tax deduction and which incentivizes individuals to buy insurance is recommended by the interviewee. This is an expert opinion piece and not research. The interviewee's conclusions are against single-payer system. The implication of his recommendations for nursing and patients is unclear. The commentator's point of view is primarily economics and not universal coverage.

Article 5:

Cooper, R. A. (2009). States with more health care spending have better-
        quality health care: Lessons about Medicare. *Health Affairs*, *28*(1),
        103-w115.

This article describes the correlation between healthcare spending and
quality of care. One conclusion is that states with more spending per capita
(from all sources) experience a higher level of quality of care. According
to the authors, quality results from the volume of spending and not
from a single-payer. Quality also correlates with other sociodemographic
context. These conclusions may refocus thinking about the impact of
health care spending, as politicians and the public continue to address
the competing issues in health care reform – including the single-payer
concept.

This systematic review considered data from a variety of government
and private sources, which were collected and analyzed in a variety of
methods. However, the article states no opinion on a single-payer system.
Nursing and patient implications are clear if the research results in more
healthcare spending – whether in the form of a single-payer system or not.
More patient care and more nursing opportunities should be expected.

Article 6:

Feldman, R. (2009). Quality of care in single-payer and multipayer health
        systems. *Journal of Health Politics, Policy & Law*, *34*(4), 649-670.
        doi:10.1215/03616878-2009-019

This article attempts to determine if Americans should expect the quality of care in a single-payer health care system to be greater than in a system such as that currently in place in America. The author concludes that single-payer systems fail to respond to demand for high quality without imposing waiting lists and that public subsidy would be a better solution. This authoritative opinion by a professor of health economics draws from a variety of public and private sources, suggesting that patients would be willing to pay substantial amounts of money to reduce waiting lines. The conclusions reached by the author do not support a single-payer system. Failure to implement a single-payer system, according to this study, would do nothing to provide more individuals with healthcare and would do nothing to increase opportunities for more nurses.

Article 7:

Glied, S. (2009). Single payer as a financing mechanism. *Journal of Health Politics, Policy & Law, 34*(4), 593-615. doi:10.1215/03616878-2009-017

The author of this study examined the amount and quality of healthcare per dollar of spending in several countries. Administrative expenses were seen as a contributor to inefficiency in the American system and the author cites several reasons to recommend a single-payer system. This descriptive research utilizes data from the Organization for Economic Co-operation and Development to contrast the quality and cost results in 18 developed countries as compared to the United States. The author's conclusions support a single-payer system. Any single-payer system will expand the availability of care to people presently uninsured and will open new job opportunities for nurses.

Article 8:

Gottlich, V., Nemore, P., & Chiplin Jr., A. J. (2011). Health care changes: Challenges to Medicare. *NAELA Journal, 7*(1), 11-34.

The importance of this study is its thorough, easy-to-read description of the Patient Protection and Affordable Care Act (PPACA), also known as "Obamacare". The PPACA is an important ingredient in the discussion about a single-payer system in America. The author comments on various sections of the law but no conclusions are drawn which would be helpful to this writer's proposal and no research is presented. The PPACA does extend coverage to many previously uninsured individuals which would, in turn, expand opportunities for nurses. However, the law does not specifically address single-payer.

Article 9:

Gusmano, M. K., Weisz, D., & Rodwin, V. G. (2009). Achieving horizontal equity: Must we have a single-payer health system? *Journal of Health Politics, Policy & Law, 34*(4), 617-633. doi:10.1215/03616878-2009-018

The authors examined health systems in three of the largest cities in the world to determine if horizontal equity (equal treatment for equal need) existed. New York employs a multi-payer system with many people not insured, London employs a single-payer system and Paris employs a universal coverage, multi-payer system. The authors attempted to determine if the means of payment affected horizontal equity and concluded that the number of payers has little to do with equal access to equal care but that universal coverage has a great deal to do with equal access.

This multivariate quantitative research utilized income, health status, neighborhood lived in and access to care, as the independent variables with morbidity and mortality being the dependent variables. Universal coverage does not, by itself, explain improved health conditions in certain populations. However, it is more likely to explain these improvements than does the number of payers. Thus, universal care for all is supported. Universal care in the United States would mean a new population of individuals with full access to care and new opportunities for nurses.

Article 10:

Hoffman, A. K. (2011). Three models of health insurance: The conceptual pluralism of the Patient Protection and Affordable Care Act. *University of Pennsylvania Law Review, 159*(6), 1873-1954.

This article presents a different look at health insurance - asking what, exactly, should health insurance cover. Three competing philosophies are presented with compelling arguments for each. The authors conclude that the healthcare debate in America has failed to clarify goals in terms of these arguments and until it does, there will be ambiguity. This expert opinion considers scholarly research as well as public and private commentary to yield a different perspective on the debate.

Whichever of these three principles would be embraced, or if a combination is embraced, the principles would seem to work only where the affected population is universally covered. Thus, a universal system would be an ingredient. Implementation of a new universal access system would result in new coverage for people previously uninsured. Such an expansion of access would result in new employment opportunities for nurses.

Article 11:

Hsuei-Chen, L., Ku-Chou, C., Yu-Ching, H., Chung-Fu, L., Jin-Jong, C., & Shun-Hwa, W. (2010). Inpatient rehabilitation utilization for acute stroke under a universal health insurance system. *American Journal of Managed Care, 16*(3), e67-e74.

This study examines a universal access, single-payer system in Taiwan to determine if the system ensures equal access to care. In this case, the study focused on inpatient stroke rehabilitation. This study could be relevant for a country considering the establishment of a more equitable system - such as universal access. A longitudinal, random sampled cohort study was utilized. The independent variable was a set of patients with a primary diagnosis of stroke. The dependent variable was whether or not an inpatient stroke patient received rehabilitation.

Study results concluded that rehabilitation services were equitably assessed by all groups of patients. This could suggest that a system of universal access and a single payer affords individuals equal access to care. Under such a system, patient population would increase and opportunity for nursing employment would improve.

Article 12:

Ke, X., Evans, D., Carrin, G., Aguilar-Rivera, A., Musgrove, P., & Evans, T. (2007) Protecting households from catastrophic health spending. *Health Affairs, 26*(4), 972-983.

This study was conducted on the significant number of individuals who do not receive care because of inadequate financial resources or those who suffer financial catastrophe due to the expense. A conclusion was reached that moving away from out-of-pocket expense to prepayment lowers the risk of financial catastrophe. This is a result in a universal access, single-payer system.

A regression analysis of a sample comparing patients in three socioeconomic groups with characteristics of subsets of individuals experiencing financial catastrophe showed that there is a negative correlation between financial catastrophe and the extent a country prepays its healthcare costs through insurance or taxes. This could lead to a conclusion that a universal system mitigates against financial catastrophe for individuals in the country adopting the system. Nurses and patients would both benefit by opening opportunities for employment and healthcare.

Article 13:

Korda, R. J., Clements, M. S., & Kelman, C. W. (2009). Universal health care no guarantee of equity: Comparison of socioeconomic inequalities in the receipt of coronary procedures in patients with acute myocardial infarction and angina. *BMC Public Health*, *9*,460-471. doi:10.1186/1471-2458-9-460

This multivariate cohort study addresses whether or not healthcare equity is assured in the universal healthcare system in Australia. The patient population in one study consisted of patients admitted with acute myocardial infarction and the other study consisted of patients admitted with angina. In each case, the independent variable was socioeconomic status and the dependent variable was receipt of specific treatments.

The study concluded that universal access does not assure that treatment is equitable across economic lines and, in fact, may actually perpetuate the inequity. This is not a result that supports a universal access, single-payer system to assure equal access to care. There are few implications for nursing from this study. Patients, on the other hand, are found to have some access to care limited because of economic circumstances.

Article 14:

Landers, R. M., & Leeman, P. A. (2011). Medicaid expansion under the 2010 health care reform legislation: The continuing evolution of Medicaid's central role in American health care. *NAELA Journal*, *7*(1), 143-164.

This article addresses the changes in Medicaid law arising from the PPACA. These changes extend Medicaid to more individuals by removing the non-income qualifying criteria. Thus, Medicaid is now fully income driven. The authors also observe that the United States is the only industrialized nation in the world not to have adopted a universal system of healthcare. The conclusion is reached that removing non-financial qualifying criteria from Medicaid eligibility moved the country closer to a single-payer system – which the authors recommend.

The report is a systematic review of various descriptive studies on Medicaid funding, eligibility and obstacles to implementation. The review gives support to the single-payer, universal access concept. Under such a program, nursing employment opportunities would improve as would patient access to care.

Article 15:

Landry, M., Williams, A., Verrier, M., Holyoke, P., Zakus, D., & Deber, R. (2008). Shifting sands: Assessing the balance between public, private not-for-profit and private for-profit physical therapy delivery in Ontario, Canada. *Physiotherapy Research International, 13*(3), 189-199.

This Canadian study addresses physical therapy treatment in public and private facilities. Because Canada is a universal access, single-payer system, where most care is delivered by the private sector, the study is important to help understand if there is any shift from not-for-profit to for-profit service providers. Such a shift is perceived to have a negative effect on the health status of the population.

This research is a case study which relies on published government data and a subjective questionnaire obtained by the researchers. No conclusion regarding the single-payer system was reached. The study could have relevance if further research showed a shift toward for-profit providers in other areas of healthcare. There is no impact to nursing or patients from this study.

Article 16:

McCormick, D., Woolhandler, S., Bose-Kolanu, A., Germann, A., Bor, D. H., & Himmelstein, D. U. (2009). United States physicians' views on financing options to expand health insurance coverage: A national survey. *JGIM: Journal of General Internal Medicine, 24*(4), 526-531. doi:10.1007/s11606-009-0916-x

This is a survey conducted by physicians among physicians designed to elicit opinion on various healthcare reform concepts including universal care. Forty-two percent favored a government-run, taxpayer-financed single-payer national health insurance program while only nine percent favored the current system. Eighty-nine percent believed individuals should receive necessary care regardless of ability to pay.

This cohort study used regression analysis to evaluate the levels of physician sentiment for each of three models of healthcare financing. This report supporting universal access and single-payer financing has implications for the political process as physicians are an important constituent in the debate. Nurses benefit from universal access by increasing the population of patients while patients benefit by gaining access to care.

Article 17:

Newhouse, J., & Sinaiko, A. (2007). Can multi-payer financing achieve single-payer spending levels? *Forum for Health Economics & Policy*, *10*(1), 1-11.

In a review of data from the Organisation for Economic Co-operation and Development (OECD), this article addresses the contention that a more centralized payment system, such as the single-payer, would result in a reduction of overall healthcare spending. Doubt is raised about the argument that administrative savings in a single-payer system are an important part of the difference in health spending levels between the United States and other countries. This descriptive study utilized data from the United States and other countries to understand spending levels and the reasons for differences.

A conclusion reached by the authors is that implementing a single-payer system in the United States would not necessarily lower the administrative costs of managing such a system. Implications for nurses and patients because of this research depend upon whether a universal access system would be implemented in spite of the results. If so, patient access to care would improve and nursing opportunities would increase.

Kim Nielsen

Article 18:

O'Neill, J., & O'Neill, D. (2007). Health status, health care and inequality: Canada vs. the United States *Forum for Health Economics & Policy*, *10*(1), 1-46.

This article questions whether the single-payer system in Canada delivers better outcomes and more fairly distributes health resources than the American system. Findings suggest the Canadian system, a single payer health system very different from the system in America, does not deliver better outcomes. Differences in infant mortality and life expectancy outcomes are not attributable to the system. This systematic review examined government-provided data from both countries to establish 15 measurements of quality and outcomes. Each was designed to contrast results between the two distinct systems.

Among the conclusions was that Americans are more satisfied with quality and outcomes than Canadians. Lack of access in America is an economic problem which is much easier to address than the problem of lack of access because of waiting lists in the Canadian system. The study argues against a single-payer alternative to the American system. The nursing and patient populations do not gain additional benefit if the status quo is maintained.

Article 19:

Strandberg-Larsen, M., & Krasnik, A. (2008). Does a public single payer system deliver integrated care? A national survey study among professional stakeholders in Denmark. *International Journal of Integrated Care (IJIC)*, 8,e61.

This study concluded that the formally integrated healthcare delivery system in Denmark does not deliver fully integrated services – a goal of the delivery system. Denmark, whose system is similar to that of the U.K. and Norway, is a single-payer, universal access health system provided for all residents. It is financed, primarily, through progressive taxation and delivered through a large public system. Surveys were conducted among various managers, administrators and physicians to evaluate whether they believed care to be coordinated.

The conclusions reached by the study, if implemented, should improve the coordination of care. Although this is a single-payer, universal system, the delivery model is not one being contemplated in the United States. Implementing the recommended changes would improve healthcare for patients but have little impact on the practice of nursing.

Article 20:

Tanner, M. (2008). *Policy analysis. The grass is not always greener: A look at national health care systems around the world.* Retrieved November 2, 2011, from CATO Institute Web site: http://www.cato.org/pubs/pas/pa-613.pdf

This author examines healthcare systems in Europe, Canada and the United States. Eleven separate healthcare financing and delivery systems of all types are described in detail. The study specifically examines a proposed single-payer system in the United States and reviews the Canadian system, which the author concludes is not a valid model for the United States. This is a descriptive study which looks at the details of various financing and delivery systems and relates them to World Health Organization data. The author concludes that improvement in quality and availability of healthcare will result more from competitive market mechanisms than government involvement. The conclusion does not argue for or against universal coverage but clearly endorses more consumer incentives and control. Implementation of the conclusions in this study would have no specific impact on nursing or patient care.

References

Baiardini, I., Bousquet, P. J., Brzoza, Z., Canonica, G. W., Compalati, E., Fiocchi, A…& Braido, F. (2009). Recommendations for assessing patient-reported outcomes and health-related quality of life in clinical trials on allergy: A GA^{2}LEN taskforce position paper. *Allergy, 65*,290–295.

Barr, D. A. (2007). A research protocol to evaluate the effectiveness of public-private partnerships as a means to improve health and welfare systems worldwide. *American Journal of Public Health, 97*(1), 19-25. doi:10.2105/AJPH.2005.075614

Bentley, T., Effros, R., Palar, K., & Keeler, E. (2008). Waste in the United States health care system: A conceptual framework. *Milbank Quarterly, 86*(4), 629-659.

Beyan, O.D., & Baykal, N. (2010). A knowledge based search tool for performance measures in health care systems. *Journal of Medical Systems*,1-19. doi:10.1007/s10916-010-9459-2

Bitton, A., Martin, C., & Landon, B. E. (2010). A nationwide survey of patient centered medical home demonstration projects. *JGIM: Journal of General Internal Medicine, 25*(6), 584-592. doi:10.1007/s11606-010-1262-8

Buerhaus, P. I. (2010). Is United States health care evolving toward a single-payer system? An interview with health care economist Paul Feldstein, PhD. *Nursing Economic$, 28*(3), 198-201.

Cooper, R. A. (2009). States with more health care spending have better-quality health care: Lessons about Medicare. *Health Affairs*, *28*(1), 103-w115.

DeNavas-Walt, C., Proctor, B. D., & Smith, J.C. (2011). *Income, poverty, and health insurance coverage in the United States: 2010*. Retrieved November 4, 2011, from U. S. Census Bureau, Current Population Reports at: http://www.census.gov/prod/2011pubs/p60-239.pdf

Feldman, R. (2009). Quality of care in single-payer and multipayer health systems. *Journal of Health Politics, Policy & Law*, *34*(4), 649-670. doi:10.1215/03616878-2009-019

Fineout-Overholt, E., & Johnston, L. (2007). Evaluation: An essential step to the EBP process. *Worldviews on Evidence-Based Nursing*, *4*(1), 54-59.

Glied, S. (2009). Single payer as a financing mechanism. *Journal of Health Politics, Policy & Law*, *34*(4), 593-615. doi:10.1215/03616878-2009-017

Gottlich, V., Nemore, P., & Chiplin Jr., A. J. (2011). Health care changes: Challenges to Medicare. *NAELA Journal*, *7*(1), 11-34.

Grand Canyon University. (n.d.) {Electronic Document} *Lecture Four*. Retrieved on November 20, 2011, from: http://angel03.gcu.edu/section/default.asp?id=839405

Gusmano, M. K., Weisz, D., & Rodwin, V. G. (2009). Achieving horizontal equity: Must we have a single-payer health system? *Journal of Health*

Politics, Policy & Law, 34(4), 617-633. doi:10.1215/03616878-2009-018

Hoffman, A. K. (2011). Three models of health insurance: The conceptual pluralism of the Patient Protection and Affordable Care Act. *University of Pennsylvania Law Review, 159*(6), 1873-1954.

Hsuei-Chen, L., Ku-Chou, C., Yu-Ching, H., Chung-Fu, L., Jin-Jong, C., & Shun-Hwa, W. (2010). Inpatient rehabilitation utilization for acute stroke under a universal health insurance system. *American Journal of Managed Care, 16*(3), e67-e74.

Ke, X., Evans, D., Carrin, G., Aguilar-Rivera, A., Musgrove, P., & Evans, T. (2007) Protecting households from catastrophic health spending. *Health Affairs, 26*(4), 972-983.

Korda, R. J., Clements, M. S., & Kelman, C. W. (2009). Universal health care no guarantee of equity: Comparison of socioeconomic inequalities in the receipt of coronary procedures in patients with acute myocardial infarction and angina. *BMC Public Health, 9*:460-471. doi:10.1186/1471-2458-9-460

Landers, R. M., & Leeman, P. A. (2011). Medicaid expansion under the 2010 health care reform legislation: The continuing evolution of Medicaid's central role in American health care. *NAELA Journal, 7*(1), 143-164.

Landry, M., Williams, A., Verrier, M., Holyoke, P., Zakus, D., & Deber, R. (2008). Shifting sands: Assessing the balance between public, private not-for-profit and private for-profit physical therapy delivery in Ontario, Canada. *Physiotherapy Research International, 13*(3), 189-199.

Laurie H. G. (2009). Reflections on health care. *Journal of Clinical Investigation, 119*(10), 2858-2859. doi:10.1172/JC140996

Mason, A., & Monk-Turner, E. (2010). Factors shaping the decision of college students to walk or drive under the influence of alcohol: A test of rational choice theory. *Drugs: Education, prevention and policy,17*(5), 560-572. doi: 10.3109/09687630802629530

McCormick, D., Woolhandler, S., Bose-Kolanu, A., Germann, A., Bor, D. H., & Himmelstein, D. U. (2009). United States physicians' views on financing options to expand health insurance coverage: A national survey. *JGIM: Journal of General Internal Medicine, 24*(4), 526-531. doi:10.1007/s11606-009-0916-x

Medicare.gov: The official U. S. Government site for Medicare. (2011). *Who is eligible for Medicare?* Retrieved November 13, 2011, from: https://questions.medicare.gov/app/answers/detail/a_id/10/~/who-is-eligible-for-medicare percent3F

Melnyk, B., & Fineout-Overholt, E. (2011). *Evidence-based practice in nursing and healthcare: A guide to best practice.* Philadelphia: Lippincott Williams & Wilkins.

Newhouse, J., & Sinaiko, A. (2007). Can multi-payer financing achieve single-payer spending levels? *Forum for Health Economics & Policy, 10*(1), 1-11.

Office of Management and Budget. (2010). *Fiscal year 2012 budget of the United States Government.* Retrieved November 13, 2011, from: http://www.whitehouse.gov/sites/default/files/omb/budget/fy2012/assets/budget.pdf

O'Neill, J., & O'Neill, D. (2007). Health status, health care and inequality: Canada vs. the United States *Forum for Health Economics & Policy*, *10*(1), 1-46.

Simon-Tuval, T., Scharf, S., Maimon, N., Bernhard-Scharf, B., Reuveni, H., & Tarasiuk, A. (2011). Determinants of elevated healthcare utilization in patients with COPD. *Respiratory Research,12*(1):1-8.

Sperling, K. L., & Shapira, O. M. (2011). Here it comes: Defined contribution health care. *Benefits Quarterly*, *27*(1), 42-48.

Strandberg-Larsen, M., & Krasnik, A. (2008). Does a public single payer system deliver integrated care? A national survey study among professional stakeholders in Denmark. *International Journal of Integrated Care (IJIC)*, *8*,e61.

Tanner, M. (2008). *Policy analysis. The grass is not always greener: A look at national health care systems around the world.* Retrieved November 2, 2011, from CATO Institute Web site: http://www.cato.org/pubs/pas/pa-613.pdf

U. S. Department of Health and Human Services: CMS/Centers for Medicaid and Medicare Services. (2011). *CMS leadership: Office of Clinical Standards and Quality.* Retrieved on November 19, 2011,

from: http://www.cms.gov/CMSLeadership/11_Office_OCSQ.
asp#TopOfPage

U. S. Department of Health and Human Services: CMS/Centers for
Medicaid and Medicare Services. (2011). *CMS regional offices:
Regional offices overview.* Retrieved on November 13, 2011, from:
http://www.cms.gov/RegionalOffices/

Walsh, N. (2010). Dissemination of evidence into practice: Opportunities
and threats. *Primary Health Care, 20*(3), 26-30.

The World Bank: Working for a world free of poverty. (2011a) *GDP
(current US$).* Retrieved November 13, 2011, from: http://data.
worldbank.org/indicator/NY.GDP.MKTP.CD

The World Bank: Working for a world free of poverty. (2011b). *Health
expenditure, total (percent of GDP).* Retrieved November 13, 2011,
from: http://data.worldbank.org/indicator/SH.XPD.TOTL.ZS

Appendix A

DeNavas-Walt, Proctor, & Smith, (2011)

Figure 7.
Number Uninsured and Uninsured Rate: 1987 to 2010

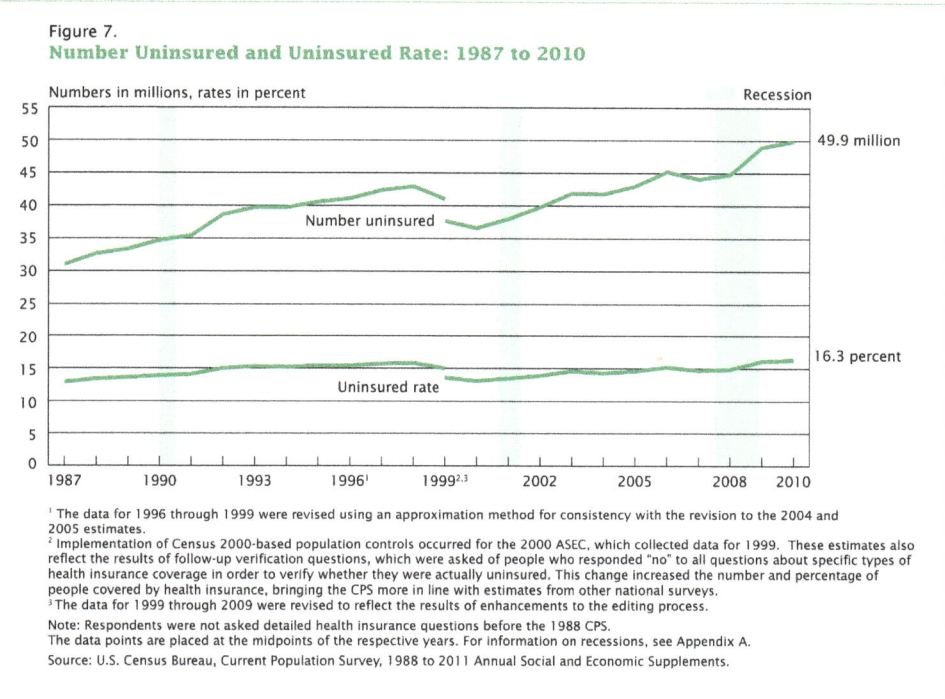

Numbers in millions, rates in percent

Number uninsured

Uninsured rate

49.9 million

16.3 percent

Recession

[1] The data for 1996 through 1999 were revised using an approximation method for consistency with the revision to the 2004 and 2005 estimates.
[2] Implementation of Census 2000-based population controls occurred for the 2000 ASEC, which collected data for 1999. These estimates also reflect the results of follow-up verification questions, which were asked of people who responded "no" to all questions about specific types of health insurance coverage in order to verify whether they were actually uninsured. This change increased the number and percentage of people covered by health insurance, bringing the CPS more in line with estimates from other national surveys.
[3] The data for 1999 through 2009 were revised to reflect the results of enhancements to the editing process.
Note: Respondents were not asked detailed health insurance questions before the 1988 CPS.
The data points are placed at the midpoints of the respective years. For information on recessions, see Appendix A.
Source: U.S. Census Bureau, Current Population Survey, 1988 to 2011 Annual Social and Economic Supplements.

U.S. Census Bureau   Income, Poverty, and Health Insurance Coverage in the United States: 2010 **23**

Appendix B

(Tanner, 2008)

Comparison of Healthcare Access, Financing and Delivery in 10 Major Industrialized
Countries

Country	Universal Access	Financing Method	Delivery System
United States	No (excluding poor and over age 65)	Multi-payer (government, employers, private pay)	Private (excluding V.A.)
Canada	Yes	Single-payer (administered by provinces)	Primarily private (long waiting lists)
United Kingdom	Yes	Single-payer	Public (most are government employees; long waiting lists)
France	Yes	Single-payer (high co-pays)	Private

Country	Universal Access	Financing Method	Delivery System
Italy	Yes	Single-payer	Public and private (widespread waiting; substandard care in public hospitals)
Japan	Yes	Multi-payer	Private (government sets all fees so feels like government system)
Norway	Yes	Single-payer	Public and Private (government delivers primary, private delivers specialty; limited physician choice; long waiting lists)

Country	Universal Access	Financing Method	Delivery System
The Netherlands	Yes (everyone must purchase insurance)	Multi-payer (individuals pay insurance companies)	Private
Switzerland	Yes (everyone must purchase insurance)	Multi-payer (individuals pay insurance companies with government subsidy)	Private
Germany	Yes	Multi-payer (individuals earning $60,000 or more pay insurance company with government subsidy; others, the government pays direct)	Private (all reimbursement rates are set by government; general strike of physicians in 2005)

APPENDIX C
Nurse Staffing Report

1. Facility Name: _____

2. Address: _____

3. Phone/Fax/email: _____

4. Taxpayer ID number: _____

5. Hospital_____ Medical group_____

    Other_____

(Describe)

6. Month_____ Year_____ of report

7. Number of nurses employed on last day of reporting period_____

8. Number of nurses added during reporting period_____

9. For *each* new nurse

    Age _____

    Specialty _____

10. Number of nurses terminated during reporting period_____

11. For *each* terminated nurse

    Age _____

    Specialty _____

    Length of service _____

12. Individual completing report

    a. Printed name _____

    b. Signature _____

To be submitted to:

Centers for Medicare and Medicaid Services Regional Office

Centers for Medicare & Medicaid Services

7500 Security Boulevard

Baltimore, MD 21244

www.ingramcontent.com/pod-product-compliance
Lightning Source LLC
Chambersburg PA
CBHW051149120626
46547CB00012B/1014